I know you KNOW

but you don't UNDERSTAND

A workbook containing

simple exercises *and* **true stories**
of
Small Business Owners *who became* **fed up**
with
Struggling, Sacrificing & Settling for Less

M. Lynne Jacob

BALBOA.
PRESS

A DIVISION OF HAY HOUSE

Balboa Press books may be ordered through booksellers or by contacting:

Balboa Press
A Division of Hay House
1663 Liberty Drive
Bloomington, IN 47403
www.balboapress.com
1-(877) 407-4847

ISBN: 978-1-4525-4482-3 (sc)
ISBN: 978-1-4525-4483-0 (e)

Because of the dynamic nature of the Internet, any web addresses or links contained in this book may have changed since publication and may no longer be valid. The views expressed in this work are solely those of the author and do not necessarily reflect the views of the publisher, and the publisher hereby disclaims any responsibility for them.

The author of this book does not dispense medical advice or prescribe the use of any technique as a form of treatment for physical, emotional, or medical problems without the advice of a physician, either directly or indirectly. The intent of the author is only to offer information of a general nature to help you in your quest for emotional and spiritual well-being. In the event you use any of the information in this book for yourself, which is your constitutional right, the author and the publisher assume no responsibility for your actions.

Any people depicted in stock imagery provided by Thinkstock are models,
and such images are being used for illustrative purposes only.
Certain stock imagery © Thinkstock.

Printed in the United States of America

Balboa Press rev. date: 02/08/2012

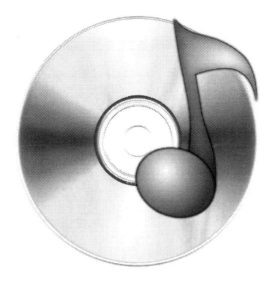

This book is also available in audio format, read by the author with the author's passion for helping you, too, receive the results available to you through her teachings.

This audio version is available to you **at no extra cost.** You are encouraged to download it and listen to it while reading and working through this workbook. It's also a great companion for you as you're driving … around town or on those long trips.

Studies have shown that studying by both reading <u>and</u> listening at the same time, dramatically enhances *and quickens* your absorption of the material you're learning.

To download your MP3 copy of this book, follow the step-by-step instructions at

<u>www.I-Know-You-Know.mljcoaching.com</u>

What STRUGGLE Actually Is

Once we cross the bridge and truly UNDERSTAND this there's no excuse for ever struggling again!

Following a ¼-century career as a legal assistant & office manager in law firms, Lynne Jacob picked up a trade and went out on her own . . . much like small business owners the world over. After a few years of living in other cultures, Lynne found *Professional Coaching* on her path. It was an instant fit for Lynne, offering her a way to live her passion, by helping families, and enjoy a comfortable living doing so. Like most small business owners, Lynne became self-employed with her trade. That was in 2003.

During the first 2 years in business, Lynne worked with a professional coach *every single week*. Rather than going to business school while operating her business, Lynne studied everything she could get her hands on. She continues to study and invest in herself through continually having her own coach, as well as working with coaching mentors, and *MLJ Coaching International* has blossomed nicely.

For a few years MLJ Coaching International was doing very well—helping several 100s of small business owners, especially those in the construction industry, after Lynne's experience as a general contractor building her home during her 2nd year of being self-employed.

In 2007 Lynne's first two grandbabies were born—5 weeks apart—and both of Lynne's daughters and their families lived 2 provinces away. For a short period Lynne's heart was broken due to the distance . . . until she constructed her 2008 1-year business plan. That year, executing her plan, Lynne saw her grandbabies in every calendar month . . . and then some!

But by the end of that fabulous year, where Lynne's sales &
profits had more than doubled while she had TONS of FUN . . . she was tired.

Lynne's business was now in its 6th year and while it didn't seem she was settling for less or sacrificing her personal or family time for the business, Lynne started experiencing some of the struggle she was hearing so much about from her more seasoned entrepreneurial clients. Lynne simply made a decision to do something about this—quickly—and within a very few months Lynne saw what the problem was . . . as well as the solution.

Through various programs focusing on her **7 Simple Strategies 4 Success**, Lynne was sharing all of the "business" knowledge she'd acquired since starting her business and combined it with the mindset coaching that small business owners need in order to succeed. Since 2009, however, Lynne has become acutely—even painfully—aware of what this **struggle** is that all small business owners experience as their businesses start to enjoy handsome growth.

Like for Lynne, most self-employed people stay self-employed, even though they may acquire employees to help leverage their time. As you'll see in Strategy #5, inside this book, one of the biggest challenges a self-employed person has is handing the reins over to the employees. **Why is that so difficult?**

As with Lynne, it was not only her best year yet when she started to struggle, because every year was better than the year before—PROFITS and FUN-wise.

It was when Lynne enjoyed phenomenal growth that she started to struggle.

Struggle: We don't even know what it is we're struggling with and therein lies the problem. Struggle appears to us to be caused by the economy, the market, the employees, the customers, the competition, the outsourcing overseas, the bankers, and so many more factors. Only when we come to know what we're actually struggling with, what the beast looks like and how to overcome it will we ever truly be able to enjoy

MORE PROFIT, TONS more FUN and RETIREMENT on your terms!

Until we overpower this beast we will continue to have one or the other, at best. We'll enjoy more profit . . . but at the cost of struggling, settling for less, sacrificing our personal and family time for the business. At times we'll increase our FUN factor, and rationalize the fact that we didn't make that much money that year . . . but it was FUN, and after all, isn't that what's most important in life? Or the fun comes from incorporating new services or products in your business, or acquiring or starting another branch of your business, and you find yourself again sacrificing your personal and family time for this growth.

Throughout these pages you're going to learn what ***struggle*** truly is . . . and why you continue to struggle. Best of all, you're going to learn how to step past this beast with which you struggle. You'll learn these **7 *Simple Strategies 4 Success*** which, when focused on and followed through with consistently & persistently, will help you, too,

TRIPLE* your *PROFITS
QUADRUPLE (at least) ***your FUN***
***Custom-Build* RETIREMENT** . . . *on **your** terms!*

And after starting to struggle in her business in that year when Lynne's sales & profits doubled, she struggled for another year until the moment when she came to ***really understand*** what struggle is and finished out that year by not doubling, nor tripling, nor even quadrupling her sales & profits. That year . . .

Lynne's sales & profits more than QUINTUPLED!!!
And she was having more FUN in her business that year than ever before!

And this is precisely what Lynne wants for you, which is why this book is much more than an informational book or a good read. This is a workbook. Dare to work through the exercises and you ***will*** turn your business around . . . completely around.

Enjoy!

INTRODUCTION

Why did You EVER go into business for Yourself IN THE FIRST PLACE?

Are you one of the millions of individuals who once thought: *I don't have to work for somebody else. I can do this myself! Just imagine all the freedom I'll have from being self-employed. I'll be the one calling the shots, choosing the customers, making SERIOUS money! Just think of the lifestyle I'll be able to provide for my spouse and children if I do this right and become really successful at this business idea I have. Just think of all the good I can do in my community (the world), by giving back, when I reach that level of disposable income.*

And are you one of the millions of small business owners who, after some 2 to 20 years, is now asking yourself ***Why did I EVER go into business for myself IN THE FIRST PLACE?***

By applying the exercises in this book you, too, can **get back in touch with your original enthusiasm** and . . .

- **Strengthen** the foundation of your business (similar to the foundation of a building);
- **Improve** *the way things are done;* and
- **Grow** your business systematically in a way that your business will sustain its growth and continue to grow, offering you many more options for the future.

The experiences you will have while following through on the exercises in this book will awaken you to the Awareness of your Operating System—that which controls your every move. And with consistent, persistent action you, too, will get to the place where you are enjoying the results that seem to elude you today. I am honoured to be there to welcome you into the *Land of Understanding.* Thank you . . . and Welcome*!*

Do you know where your business will be 3 years from today? How certain are you?

The market is full of good books on how you can improve the way you run your business, get out of debilitating debt, save for the future, plan for handing the business down to your children, sell your business outright, etc. These books are great for planting seeds in your mind of how things "could" be *if only* . . .

It's my burning desire that this book be vastly different. *7 **Simple Strategies** that carried **SMALL BUSINESS OWNERS** from **STRUGGLING** to **QUINTUPLING** their **PROFITS** in under 2* years **without** working **Harder, Longer Hours**, which I might have called this book, is much more than an informational book or a good read. This is a workbook. Dare to work through the exercises and you ***will*** turn your business around . . . completely around.

I have included herein many case studies of my clients, as well as some of the very exercises included in ***MLJ Coaching International*** coaching programs where clients invest $2,000 to $120,000/year. You will see how all of these people and 1000s more have gone from being frustrated, overwhelmed, and disillusioned with their current business results, and from struggling for more, settling for less, and sacrificing most of their personal and family life for the business to:

- tripling their PROFITS or better (in some cases, much better than quintuple);
- at least quadrupling their FUN by quadrupling their annual vacations in the first 6 months of an MLJ Coaching International program, and taking longer vacations than they ever imagined possible; as well as
- building RETIREMENT . . . on their terms, by
  - acquiring properties—residential or small commercial—for rental income;
  - acquiring or starting other businesses that complement theirs;
  - hiring and developing Operations Managers who may purchase the business from them;
  - purchasing or building commercial complexes where they'll rent their premises from their own holding company and rent out the other units; etc.

The examples are numerous and the possibilities are as great as the list of clients I have the immense pleasure of serving.

How many small business owners do you know of who put off their dream vacations and dream adventures until they *retire*, and then either don't even make it to retirement or when they do, they fear outliving their money, so they can't possibly spend it frivolously on *having FUN*?

Throughout these pages you're going to learn my *7 Simple Strategies 4 Success* which, when focused on and followed through with consistently & persistently, will help you

TRIPLE your PROFITS
QUADRUPLE (at least) your FUN
Build RETIREMENT . . . on your terms!

This book can help you be successful: IF you simply make a DECISION to *work through* this book and *complete the exercises* contained herein, and IF you FOLLOW THROUGH on that decision ("IF" being the operative word), then you, too, WILL enjoy the types of benefits that 1000s of other small business owners are enjoying today.

I look forward to hearing about your changes to *the way things are done around here* and your successes and am here for you if you want more directed guidance in the process.

Here's to your Success!

Lynne Jacob

> *NOTE:* While the clients' results referred to throughout this entire book are actual results and are equally possible for everyone, they are not guaranteed.

CHAPTER ONE

Be Open to the Possibilities!

Your Mind is Like a Computer Operating System

The only limits in this world are in our minds—our feeling minds. Our feeling mind (the subconscious mind) is understood by so few people, yet it functions like the Operating System in your computer. Do you truly know how Windows or Mac OS work? So very few people do. Even computer repair folks don't understand *how* they work. Most just know how to work *with* them.

A computer's Operating System can be turned off. Our own personal Operating Systems, on the other hand, NEVER shut down. They're even stronger when we're sleeping. Just think of some of the dreams you've had.

Every feeling we ever have—good or bad—comes from our Operating System. Our feelings are then processed by our thinking mind (conscious mind) and it's from there that we make our decisions. This means that every decision we make, depending on the amount of time we "think about" the idea, is based on our feelings about it.

And get this: Every feeling we have is a memory. Do you get that?

Consider this: We can't possibly have a feeling about something that we've never done before—about an experience we've never had before. Yet we have "feelings" about **everything!**

This means that whenever we have a conscious thought about doing or acquiring something new, our subconscious mind/Operating System is bringing up a feeling from a past incident that "seems to be" similar to this new opportunity/idea. Our subconscious mind now *paints* this new idea with past emotions and there we are . . . Making decisions based on experiences from our past, and often bringing up the emotion of fear. That means that pretty much every decision we ever make—in business and everywhere—is based on the past. How successful can that be?

The Natural Resources of Your Business

Of all of the resources in the world, to date I have found only one that is truly limited on this plane and that is TIME. Those 60 seconds tick by every single minute whether you are constructive, productive, neutral, or destructive with your actions during that period. You'll never get those seconds back—none of them. On the other hand, money (the second resource) is actually *unlimited*. I know that may feel questionable at the moment, but let's just say you do believe this statement for the purposes of enjoying the benefits available to you through this book.

The third major resource for your business, and in life in general, is Humans. They, too, are unlimited. We make more of them every minute. Would you agree with me, therefore, that TIME is the only common resource that is limited?

That said, I'm sure you want to make the best use of TIME as is possible. This doesn't mean that you are like the Tasmanian devil in the cartoons, spinning in circles. Rather, it means that when you have a desire, you take action on realizing that desire immediately, before the feeling mind has time to negatively influence your thinking mind and cause you to second-guess your desire. If time truly is limited, then you want to spend a minimal amount of it weighing pros and cons over decisions. Nor do you want to spend your time struggling, sacrificing, and settling for less than what you now know you deserve to receive.

Making the best use of TIME also means that you and I want tangible results in our businesses and therefore, we want tangible results in our clients' businesses. Isn't that true for you? That's a challenge for us, at times, because many small business owners can't measure their results.

Clients tell me they just want LESS of what they don't want, and MORE of what they do. As you'll read in Strategy #4, you'll see that it's essential for success to *know your numbers*.

Get Tough. No Messing Around!

My clients describe me as being a *tell-it-like-it-is* person, as being strict yet kind. I'm not looking for compliments. I'm looking for tangible results for my clients. I very much want you to

- triple your profits and income if that's what you want;
- take 3-week vacations in the middle of your busiest season;
- take 4 vacations each year in order to have more fun and to be fully recharged in your business;
- play hooky with your children to go skiing (or whatever your family loves to do) on a slow day at work;
- go from struggling with time, organization, cash-flow and profits, to enjoying 10 times the profit you were earning before we met, in less than 2 years.

That's right: **10 times!** This is why my clients are put into the hot-seat when I'm hearing them complain about an employee for the second or third time. I've been known to ask: *Why the heck is (s)he still there?* This is why, when I hear a client telling me how busy (s)he is and therefore was unable to follow through on something—for example, the sales tactics—I say: *Without sales you have no business. Call me back when you've called that prospect.*

I call myself a server of tough love. It helps my clients become owners of successful businesses and to become championship leaders in their businesses, as well as in their families and personal lives.

So, as you're reading through these pages if/when you come across some concepts that sound kind of hokey or woo-woo, trust me: They are neither! It's for your benefit to start learning these things because it's precisely this stuff that you're not aware of that's going on every second in every day in your Operating System that's holding you back. It's your Operating System that keeps you playing small. I know this so well, because, even though I was already an expert at helping my clients triple their beneficial business results, I was still subject to the workings of my own Operating System.

As you read this stuff, if you find yourself rolling your eyes, set the book down. Have a talk with yourself, saying something like:

> *Look, Joe. You may not get this right now, but 1000s of other small business owners were open-minded enough to at least go with it and they turned their businesses completely around. Your family deserves this and for that matter, Joe, you deserve this, too. So open your mind and go back and reread that paragraph and allow it to sink in. You don't have to believe it, just go with it. Let's see what happens.*

You may want to print that out and slip it inside one of the covers of this book or flag this page, because you're apt to roll your eyes a few times. Ask any of my clients. Ask my friends and family members!

What's more important to you?

a) Following people who are also settling for less while struggling for more?
b) Being accepted by everyone?
c) Or having TONS of FUN today and a lucrative RETIREMENT allowing you TONS more FUN later?

These experiences form the **bridge** from **Knowledge** to **Understanding**. You're currently on that bridge, albeit just at the beginning of it, where you're applying all of the knowledge you've acquired to this point to run a business—in that place where you find yourself saying "Yes, I know. I know that." Yet somehow, even though you "know" about running a successful business, because you were successful up to a certain point, you just can't seem to get past this point. Today you find yourself in a nearly constant state of **Struggle and Frustration.** You're stuck at the beginning of this bridge . . . on your way to the land of **Understanding**— understanding your Operating System, which is the main operating system in your business. After all, if you are the sole proprietor of your business, you are your business and your business is you.

Throughout all of the exercises in this book, you, too, can continue along this bridge instead of turning back to the land of **Knowledge** as 99 in every 100 business owners do in the 1st 9 years of business, where you feel comfortable because "you know" what you need to do even though you find yourself struggling and sacrificing . . . and worse yet, settling for less. Throughout the exercises contained in this book you, too, can bridge that gap between **Knowledge** and **Understanding,** which gap, at times, feels to be the size of the St. Lawrence River.

May this book serve to be a bridge above that canyon. With proper support, you, too, can keep going all the way across that bridge as the many people, about whom you'll read in this book, have done.

CHAPTER TWO

Choose your Destination—Any Destination!

Strategy # 1:
DESIGN YOUR CREATION: Construct a Compelling 3-year Vision

While reviewing this book before sending it off to the publisher I was leaving a 3-month vacation of touring around the Eastern half of Australia in a campervan. *Talk about FUN!* On my way to the airport the driver started up a conversation. Being who I am, I asked him a few questions about his business, business results, joy of being in business, what he'd *really* like to do if he had no limitations, restrictions or obstacles stopping him. Pretty usual conversation for me. He became very interested in the way in which I serve the world from the questions I was asking him and he delightedly shared a lot of his "business woes" with me in a short period.

I explained to him the value of getting in touch with his true desire, his passion, his purpose . . . and to live his life through serving others through his purpose. Now, I want you to understand me clearly. Owning a limousine service is a fabulous way to serve the world . . . but this fellow only scored it as 6/10 on how much he enjoyed it. I explained: *Instead of putting me into the backseat of your vehicle, seating yourself behind the steering wheel and driving around hoping you will eventually find the airport, why not map out the route by using the tools available to you, such as a map or a GPS?*

He instantly became so excited as this light-bulb of **understanding** turned on for him. *"That's what I've been doing for years,"* he said *"and that's what I was just talking about doing again! Now I get it! You're right. This is why, as you say, we need*

> *to INVEST in OURSELVES so we can find our destination and then only go in that direction."*

Yes, he was absolutely correct. He did get it!

The value of knowing where your business is headed, where it's going, what the "end goal" is, is one of those intangible results. The way we measure it, however, becomes tangible. One of the biggest components of having a 3-year Vision is the excitement and joy it invokes in you, and the motivation and enthusiasm it elicits to help you in dealing with the **day-to-day** "running" of your business. In this section of the book you'll learn how to construct *your very own COMPELLING 3-year Vision*—**a non-traditional Business Plan**.

It's essential to stay focused on TODAY'S results, even though we're looking at 3 years down the road, and we'll be managing and focusing on today's results throughout the following 6 Strategies. Your 3-year vision helps you KNOW—not just hope, but KNOW—where your business and you will be 3 years from today. KNOWING your destination will give you the strength, the encouragement, the motivation, and most importantly: **the pleasure** of doing *whatever the heck it takes* to reach your destination.

One of the most important pieces of advice I can give you towards reaching your 3-year Vision . . . while
- dramatically increasing profits today,
- being in control of your cash-flow,
- getting the FUN back into your business TODAY and especially into your life outside of the business and even
- saying YES to all of those opportunities that will be coming down the pipes to help you build RETIREMENT . . . on your terms . . .

is to LINK EVERYTHING you do . . . EVERYTHING . . . to your 3-year vision—your non-traditional Business Plan.

For many of us sole-proprietors, with and without staff/employees, as well as partnerships, a business plan is merely a document required to get a loan or an operating line of credit—in order to get started in business maybe, to take that leap of faith in growing your business by acquiring a building to take your small business out of your home, to purchase a major piece of equipment, to enable you to step into the bigger arena by having a sizeable Operating Line of Credit, etc.

When was the last time you looked at your Business Plan? If you're one of the few who have reviewed it within the last year, how up-to-date and accurate is it today? Maybe you're like me and you have never created a "traditional" business plan, yet you're feeling somewhat afraid of one day being forced to produce one, thereby having to hire a consultant to do one *for* you—one that will fly with the Bank.

My business plan was created **by me** just before I started my business . . . before I knew anything about the "traditional" business plan. In fact, when asked about a business plan, it invoked queasy feelings in the pit of my stomach. Back then I didn't really know what a Business Plan was. It just seemed to be something "officious" required by government or banks. Hence the queasy feelings, right? I've since learned that one only needs a traditional business plan if you want to "invite others into your business."

However, should you wish to SUCCEED in your business . . . really SUCCEED in the way you secretly hope and dream success to be, you **MUST** have a **non-traditional business plan**—the most powerful business plan going. The proof I offer you is in the number of sole-proprietors and "small" partnerships who don't even think of their traditional business plans once the Plans served their purpose in helping them get that loan. More proof is the number of sole-proprietors and partnerships that "intended" to be at a certain bench-mark by now, but aren't even close and aren't sure even now how they'll get there . . . or if they ever will.

Worst of all, is that about 80% of small business owners did have a business plan created—a *traditional* one—yet still only 1 in every 100 small businesses survives year 9, making it to year 10.

You read that correctly. I gathered that statistical information in 2003. As of the time of writing this book, after all these years, current statistics *still* show that a full 90% of small businesses cease to exist by the 5th year; and then only 1 in 100—yes a mere 1% (the same % as nearly a decade ago)—are still around (and not necessarily thriving) by year 10. This means than 99% of these small businesses have become painful memories to many families—and 80% of those entrepreneurs *had* a traditional business plan.

Do I have your attention yet? How likely do you feel you would create a *non-traditional* business plan (NTBP), if you saw the steps to take towards doing it in the following pages?

Case Study

An under-40 male contractor found creating a 3-year vision for his business to be quite challenging. Not only was he extremely busy running his $750,000/year small business, but he was challenged on a daily basis with his growing team, his demanding customers, cash-flow, finding *quality* time to be with his wife and their 2 very young children. He found it extremely difficult to take 3 days *away* from everything, even the family, to allow himself some time and space in which to **dream** about where he could possibly take his business 3 years from then. With some guidance, the one and only component he could see was his business relocating into bigger space. When he shared this with me one day in a coaching session his wife exclaimed her surprise as this was the first time she'd heard of such an idea. After all, they had only built their home 3 years earlier with the shop and separate office to make things easier for both of them by running the business from their home.

To help him breathe some life into this fleeting idea, I helped him describe it with a bit more detail.

When will you and your business be operating in that bigger space?

"In 5 years' time," he stated emphatically, to his wife's surprise . . . and delight. She, too, saw that operating the business from their home wasn't what they thought it would be.

What needs to happen for that move to take place?

"Well, to start with I need to increase sales—and profit, of course."

And what are some of the steps to do that?

"Well," he reflected, "I really haven't thought it out, yet."

When could you think it out?

"Hmmmmm . . . never thought about it," he says, as a big smile comes across his face. He was already having flashes go through his mind of what this larger business in this new space looked like.

This contractor, with 5 guys in the field and 2-part time office staff, signed the lease 8 months later and on March 1st received the key for *that very space* that started flashing through his mind in that coaching session that afternoon in May, fewer than 10 full months from first discussing it and just 13 months after entering into his first ever Business Coaching partnership. In fewer than 10 months he went from merely starting to see images of his 5-year pipe-dream taking form in his mind's eye to having brought the idea all the way into the physical form. The new business space was a reality in as much time as it takes to have a baby!

It was a challenge organizing the leasehold improvements while running a quickly growing business, but in much the same way as it's challenging to deal with all of the adjustments to our lives when we bring that new baby home from the hospital, it happened, little-by-little. They moved in a few months later. Within 3 months of signing this lease, before they'd even moved in, he had picked up another customer: the entire row of commercial buildings in which his new unit is situated, because his landlord liked his personality.

He's also getting a nice ROI—Return on Investment—on his monthly rent from the inventory he's accumulating. You see, this was a big component of the "extra space". During our coaching sessions, he was seeing how much time and money that was being spent when his guys would "go shopping," nearly on a daily basis. Sure it was fun for his guys, but how productive is it when your employees have to stop in to your suppliers every morning on their way to a job-site, where they chit-chat with all the other contractors' employees who are doing their morning shopping, chatting with your suppliers' employees who are now becoming their friends, and worst of all . . . how does it affect productivity when your employee is in the midst of a job and realizes he doesn't have some material and has to pack everything up, go across town, have these "friendly" visits and pick up the one crucial piece he was missing?

In addition to minimizing the shopping for his guys, himself and his administrative assistants by constantly phoning in small orders, Len's extra space for storage also increases his buying power because he's now able to purchase in larger quantities and take advantage of sales and clear-outs. An unexpected advantage of having the loft in his new quarters, however, is that now suppliers are calling Len to see if he has a "this" or a "that" that they don't have in stock for a customer who needs it today, which they'll replace when it comes in. It puts a huge smile on Len's face each time he can "give back" to his community by providing his suppliers with whichever uncommon part they're looking for. In fact, as his business coach I asked him what he charges for this service and he said the sheer joy that he gets from being in this successful position to be able to help out is a HUGE return on his investment of having the supplies on-hand.

This NTBP (non-traditional business plan), is a plan for *you*—the business owner—made *by* you. Still today, I work from the same model of business plan and even for the $25-million companies I'm helping to strengthen, improve and grow I encourage their owners to use this format. It's all-encompassing. It's holistic. It takes everything into account—especially the business owner.

After all . . . you're the backbone of your business. Have you ever had a sore back? If so, how does the rest of your body feel when your spine's not well? How does your business feel, even, when your "backbone" is suffering? Your business is an extension of you. As much as we'd like to be able to "turn off" our business mind when we leave the business it's next to impossible to do, for any serious length of time. (I'll explain in Strategy #2 how to at least turn off your business mind for periods of time.) It's not like we can go home at the end of the day and turn off our minds as we lock that door behind us. This is precisely why our NTBP absolutely MUST include the life of the business owner, as well.

This NTBP is simple, fun and compelling. This 3-year vision draws you to it. The amazing thing is that just by having this vision in writing . . . and in pictures . . . you'll find yourself saying: *Wow! Look at that! That's already happened and I wasn't even intending to focus on it until later.* It becomes a very clear, concise picture of your future created simply by your giving yourself the time and space to *think through your own ideas*.

A good professional coach . . . be it business or life . . . helps people think through their ideas. I don't jump all over them with the "how to" create their 3-year vision; nor the "how to" realize their goals; nor the "how to" follow through; or "how to" control their finances or better lead their team or get referrals from their impressed clientele . . . nor even "how to" get a life outside of the business. Of utmost importance is that we nourish our own ideas—not others'. We've been focusing and acting on others' ideas all our lives and this is precisely why some 97% of the population is so disillusioned with their lives and with their business results.

From the time we're very little we're programmed to do what others tell us to do. Sadly, we don't change that programming and even throughout our adult lives we continue to give far more importance to *the good opinion of other people*, as Dr. Wayne Dyer refers to in *The Secrets of Manifesting your Destiny*. In order for you to enjoy the types of benefits in your life . . . **through your business**, just as you were hoping for way back in the beginning, before even going into business for yourself . . . then you simply need to start taking consistent, persistent action on *your own* ideas. After all, these ideas came to *you*—not me or anyone else. In fact, if you pay close attention you'll find that those who are so full of *good opinions* that they feel the need to shower them on others rarely take consistent, persistent action on their own ideas.

A good professional coach asks inquisitive questions about your ideas and then holds the space for the client to stay focused on "thinking it out," as Len said. Thinking an idea all the way through, so that you come out the other side of it is what so few people make the space or take the time to do.

How about you?

If you KNEW . . . or at least if you would believe for the next 3 years . . . that
- everything you want to have;
- everything you want to do; and
- whomever you want to be

were possible, and that only you and your beliefs—your operating system, as I call it—are stopping you from being, having and doing everything you want . . . **IF ONLY** you were to allow yourself to believe this,

What would your 3-year vision look like?

This is one of the biggest challenges for 97% of the population—that huge portion of the population that doesn't reach their goals and instead settles for a life of struggle, sacrificing all of their wants and desires for what they feel is their *lot in life*. In order to get ahead we feel it requires so much more struggling and sacrificing that after we step into it and it doesn't seem to work for us, we lower our goals and tell ourselves that that's good enough, anyway. At least it's better than what we had or where we were. And as one young man, 20 years old, told me just the other day: *I usually down-scale my goals because I really don't like being disappointed so reaching a small goal is better than not reaching an exciting (big) goal.* There we go again: Settling for our *lot in life*. About 3 months ago, in a VIP Intensive ½-day coaching session, a client actually used these words: *Lynne, is that too much to ask for? Am I being greedy?*

What he was asking for, what he was desirous of, was to get his business to a place where all of his bills were paid up so that his wife could and maybe would have confidence in him again. He's a skilled tradesperson and even though he'd been in business for almost 2 decades, now, it was still just him in the business working alone—on the tools and in the office.

You see, by this man not clearly knowing what his goals were—something on which to stay focused as he operated his business—he found that he was all over the place, and look where that got him. Sure they had a nice enough life, living in a nice enough home and his children have had everything they've ever wanted. All of this, however, came through struggling and sacrificing. Now their debt-load was almost too much to continue carrying. However, quitting simply isn't in this contractor's vocabulary so he made another investment—this time in himself and he's getting his debts cleared up by **knowing** where he's going, where his business is going and where he's taking his family. He's had more critical conversations with his wife and the whole family in the last 3 months than in the last 20 years. In fact, he and his wife now have weekly meetings. They take place during his business development time. He's already seeing improvement in their marriage and he feels a lot of improvement in his business mindset as he follows the simple tactics and strategies that you'll find throughout this book to grow his business. Nearing the end of his first MLJ Coaching International program, he said 7 months earlier he hadn't been doing any of these things and now he had 2 manageable payments left to make against his debts, with which he had been very heavily burdened when we first started, and then he would have but one revolving line of credit on which he owed.

How can this be?

How can it be that to simply KNOW where you're headed in your business . . . and to KNOW, or at least BELIEVE that you will succeed . . . can improve your marriage?

It's a common occurrence, in fact, for my clients to be enjoying more fun in their marriages and in their family life. With another business owner where his wife isn't involved in the business he would bounce his ideas off his wife, looking for her support. WRONG person, in this case, to get support for ideas to grow the business. She's an employee—and not in his business. She doesn't, nor can't, understand the risks a business owner takes every day. It's a risk every single day of our lives as business owners. So, whenever this man would bounce an idea off his wife she would show him only the *dangerous* side of the *"what-ifs"* and that would be enough to stop him in his tracks, feeling defeated. With the outside support of a business coach, whose only goal working with you is to help you step into SUCCESS, we look at these risks from every angle with an attitude of . . .

> *It's your idea.*
> *What needs to happen to make it a reality?*
> *What are the benchmarks you need to reach along the way to know it's a successful venture?*

As this person takes his business from super-struggling, a source of frustration, irritation and disillusionment, where he was seriously considering pulling the plug on it just 4 ½ years ago, to now doing only a few jobs each year because they're all worth over $1M, reaping a solid 10-20% profit margin, his wife is enjoying the fruits of her husband's labour instead of watching him struggle, listening to him complaining, seeing him sacrificing time with his family for more time spent struggling in the business, sometimes not even making a profit on the jobs they were performing.

Is there any wonder why their marriage is more fun, as they take the 4th 5-star vacation inside of 1 year?

I have the pleasure of working with a couple as they turn their business completely around. In less than 2 years' time they've gone from either showing a minimal profit year-after-year, or a negative one . . . and that was all thanks to their accountant being very creative . . . to now truly making a solid minimum 15% profit on each job, with extras being requested by their customers as the jobs progress. And their jobs now are much bigger than they used to be. Instead of building starter homes on speculation of selling them (wishing and hoping), they now only build pre-sold homes worth a minimum of twice as much as a starter home, yet most of the pre-sold homes range in the 3-4x as much as the spec/starter homes that used to comprise most of their business.

Do you think the lack of financial pressure might have an effect on their married life? They're both amazed at how much more fun they're having … feeling like teenagers again, holding hands as they walk down the street … on a FUN business trip, or on a couple's vacation, knowing their children are well cared-for and having fun on their sleep-overs.

These are just a few of the benefits of investing your valuable time in creating a 3-year vision.

These stories also explain why, when creating your 3-year vision for your business, you want to include every part of you in the vision. As I'm sure you're coming to understand: It's not only for the business.

You see, when we first dreamed of going into business for ourselves, or of buying the business or taking the business over from our parents so they could retire or so you could still have a job because you don't know what else you'd do (I've heard all of these stories), then in your dreams you saw you and your family *living the good life*.

How good is your life today?

Would you like it to be better?

Your business is simply a vehicle to transport you and your family from the life you have today—and I'm not saying it isn't a good enough life. What I am saying is that there's no reason to stop here. Your business is the vehicle that can transport you from your lifestyle today to the lifestyle you dream of.

Every organism on this planet is subject to the universal laws. Every organism, including humans. All of those other organisms don't fight growth and expansion. Just look at mould, for example. So why do humans struggle so?

Humans fight growth. We tell ourselves we're asking for too much because we've been programmed to believe that we should be satisfied with what we have and not be greedy.

Every organism is subject to growth and expansion. Therefore, so are we. We should be grateful for everything we have, absolutely. And we can still desire MORE, because that's a universal law. To settle for only what we have means that we will invest a lot of time and struggle to maintain what we currently have because another universal law to which every organism is subject is the Law of Polarity. This means that if our businesses and we are not growing . . . we are doing the opposite: dying. So, should you decide to *be satisfied* with what you have and stay at that stage, you will soon go back to struggling to maintain what you have, that with which you *were* satisfied.

You're no longer satisfied with it, because maintaining it is causing you to struggle again. It's at this point that many businesses become smaller and the business owner says: *I knew it was too good to be true.* In fact, the business owner caused the demise of his business because he was stopping the business from continued growth; causing the business to start dying.

And so it is for us humans, too. We, too, need to grow. After we've reached adulthood the continued growth does *not* have to be in physical size. I contend that our continued growth, once we're adults, is through **personal development**.

Our business is merely an extension of who we are, as I explained earlier referring to us being the backbones of our business. Likewise, our businesses can never be any bigger than we are. Therefore, in order to strengthen, improve and grow our businesses we must strengthen, improve and grow ourselves—through personal development.

And the place to start in strengthening your own and your business' foundation is by knowing where you're going; knowing what your business will look, act and feel like when it gets to that next stage. I warn you, however, what has happened for me and for all of my clients who take Strategy #1 seriously:

DESIGN your CREATION: Construct a Compelling 3-year Vision

is that they see almost all, if not more than all, of their 3-year vision in 2 years. I say "warn" because what then happens is that these folks are struggling again just after the 2-year mark because, as I mention above, they're following their childhood programming, and like good girls and boys they're being *satisfied* with their accomplishments and then they find themselves struggling again, feeling like they're right back where they were before they first created their first-ever 3-year vision because they're subconsciously trying to "stop the growth".

In Strategy #2 you'll learn how to deal with that. I'm simply putting the caveat in here now so you'll be sure to follow the ongoing steps, as well.

Your compelling vision: for *your* business ... and your LIFE outside of the business

"So tell me! How do I create this 3-year vision?" I'm sure you're asking by now.

It's very simple.

Simply ask yourself this question:

"On _____ [date 3 years from today] when I look back at the previous 36 months, what would have had to have happened to me, both personally and professionally, for me to be delighted with my progress?"

Now itemize all the things you want to **do,** to **have** and to **be** 3 years from now. List at least 7 items for each of the 3 categories. Really stretch yourself. We're programmed by "societal conditioning" as I call it, to think and even dream "safely". We can actually only think of and dream about things that we can SEE in our mind's eye. Very few of us allow ourselves to think and dream any bigger than that. Thankfully there are some who allow themselves to do so because they're the ones who have invented things that never before existed—people like Alexander Graham Bell, Albert Einstein, Thomas Edison, Willis Haviland Carrier, Mike Lazaridis, and millions of others. That said, even these inventions were simply **growing** things that already existed. Who knows? You may have an invention inside of yourself that you're not allowing to surface, or maybe you're simply holding yourself back from allowing your current business, which is the way in which you serve the world, to grow and prosper in ways you can't even imagine today. Therefore, as you're listing all of these items you want to have and things you want to do and be, you'll want to relate all of your desires to

- work
- finances
- family
- environment
- physical
- social/friends
- health/vitality
- emotional well-being
- fun and recreation
- intellectual
- spiritual
- and any other category you can think of and find yourself dreaming about.

It's essential that your items are truly your desires. This is not the place to include items you "should" or you "could" do, have or be. These are for you. Whenever we hear ourselves saying "I should" do that, "I could get that" then ask yourself whose voice you're hearing because, in fact, those "should"s and "could"s and "would if"s are NOT your desires. They're someone else's. Leave others' desires for them. They're likely only their desires for you, anyway. If they are truly their desires for themselves you could gift them with a copy of this book and help them realize their own dreams. This *compelling* 3-year vision will only compel you toward achieving it *if* it's truly a desire of your own.

Once you **know** what you want, you will recognize it when you receive it. When you have this document in writing, supported by picture images, reviewing it periodically (say, every 3 months) you will start to see how some of the items on your list are showing up. They're becoming a reality. What you will have on paper is what we call the "ideal life" or the "ideal business." It's just an ideal. Putting that "ideal" business and life on paper is turning your "ideals" into a plan. Just by having a plan, you'll start seeing results. **I guarantee it!** If you take the action suggested throughout this book and you don't enjoy much better business results, I'll delightfully buy your copy of this book back from you.

If you're feeling even a bit sceptical right now then go to my website **www.mljcoaching.com/testimonials/** and listen to Lionel saying how he didn't believe that reaching his strong desire of only working a 40-hour week was possible, especially because of the success of their business. It wasn't Lionel's decision to attend my seminar that day and he continued to resist believing he'd be successful during our coaching sessions. Nonetheless, he complied with Chantel's wishes and his own secret desire to reach that 40-hour work-week goal and, as you'll hear him say, within 3 months his ideal work schedule became reality. You'll even hear him say he thought I was crazy to suggest it was even possible. Well, it's been a good year-and-a-half already since we first met and Lionel is still working between 35 and 40 hours a week. How? Because **he made a decision** and even though he didn't believe it possible, he followed through on his commitment to be able to dispel his (limiting) belief . . . and he's delighted that he did!

Identify your Roles

When we're looking at all of the items you want to enjoy over the next 3 years it will serve you well to relate them to all of the different roles you play. Roles represent the key relationships you have with other people. Roles represent your principal areas of responsibility in life. Roles also represent the areas in which you can make a contribution.

List each of the roles you play or the various hats you wear. For example, you may be a spouse, parent, business owner, friend, sibling, community member, sports team member, sports coach, employer, etc. It's important to include SELF as one of the roles, as well. This is the role we seem to neglect the most yet, when out of alignment, the one that wreaks the most havoc in our businesses and in every other role we play.

You're starting to see, I'm sure, that this book is more than a resource manual, or a tool for increasing your business knowledge. If you follow these exercises, **IF** being the operative word here . . . but **IF** you follow through with these exercises I'm sharing with you, you alone can turn your business around on a dime! Therefore, I encourage you to put the book down just now and spend the rest of the time you would have in reading to acquire an attractive notebook or binder and follow along with these exercises, keeping all of your loose hole-punched sheets in your binder or, even better yet, using a bound attractive notebook. The reason I always recommend a bound workbook or binder for my clients is because you're able to refer back to this point in time . . . ***the time you finally took your business seriously*** . . . and see the journey you took from this moment onward.

Therefore, I encourage you to get a notebook or binder and complete the exercises I'm giving you throughout this book. The reason I say "attractive" is because, as the word implies, you will be "attracted" to picking up the notebook and working on it. If you only have a plain-looking notebook or binder where you currently are and are telling yourself "this'll do" then there are 2 things I want to offer you on that point.

1. That's fine. You can easily dress it up once you clarify your goals by putting pictures of them on the cover.
2. With a "this'll do" attitude towards completing these exercises which will have you working on your business success, you'll only enjoy "this'll do" results. Here's a sentence that I recommend you put on a sheet of paper and hang in your office, put on the dash of your truck, hang on your refrigerator, put on the ceiling above your bed, wherever:

   The way you do anything is the way you do everything.

   Therefore, if you have a "this'll do" attitude towards completing these exercises, I know and you should know, too, that you also have a "this'll do" attitude with everything else in your life . . . and in your business. Wouldn't you rather have an attitude of

   "If it's worth doing, it's worth doing very well?"

Back to the Roles you play. In fact, this is why Lionel (referred to above) agreed to joining Chantel to attend my seminar: Lionel was a new father, yet he was seldom or never there to see his baby and as the little one started toddling he wasn't able to enjoy many of the fun times with him. Lionel's role as a parent was his main motivation to agree to working with me.

You've now listed in your attractive notebook or on foolscap for insertion into your binder, all of the various roles you play.

For each of these roles there are key people connected to you. For example in your role as a spouse, your life partner is the key person connected to that role. In your role as a business owner, it may be your Operations Manager, your Administrative Manager, your foreman, who is the key person connected to that role. For your role as "self" these key people may change somewhat frequently, such as at one point your physical trainer may be your key person and at another time your professional or business coach may be your key person. For each of your roles, identify the key person or key people connected to you in that role.

For each of the roles you play, how would you describe your ideal performance? This likely isn't a part of your reality at the moment because there's always room for improvement in everything we do and every role we play. For each role describe your ideal performance to which you will strive. For example, using your role as parent you might write: *I share equally in the parental responsibilities, including taking my children to important events. I give my children unlimited love and support and am patient with them as they develop. I invest time in truly listening to them and make it safe for them to say anything to me. I encourage open and honest communication at all times.*

The Language we Use

As you see in the example, it's essential to use positive statements when describing our ideal performance in our roles. This is who we want to become. Because our minds take action on verbs it's important to speak in the positive, as opposed to negating the negative. *Eg. I won't lose my cool when my children tell me they've caused a problem.* Your mind, acting on the verb/action word is being instructed to lose your cool. I won't go into NLP (Neuro Linguistic Programming) here, but suffice to say that this is key to our personal and business performance and to being understood while communicating. Because our minds ACT on the ACTive verbs, investment of your attention to "saying what you mean" will reap huge rewards for you.

Do you know any people who tend to complain a lot? Are you one yourself? We all have been at certain times in our lives and, unfortunately, some people just love to be that way. The next time you hear yourself complaining, ask yourself what it is that you value that isn't happening. Which ideals do you have that aren't materializing? This makes BMWs of us (belly-achers, moaners and whiners). Create your NTBP, review it periodically and you will start to see it showing up in your business and in your life outside of the business. You'll also find yourself complaining a whole lot less, because you'll be more motivated towards having more desirable results from your business plan. You'll find yourself focusing on *what you want* (as opposed to what you don't).

To learn a little more on the use of NLP you can simply download my e-book, from Amazon, called **"Next time, would you mind asking for walls and windows?" A "how to" guide for setting FUN, outlandish goals . . . and reaching them!** In that short read I give numerous examples of the power of our spoken . . . and even unspoken words and I could give hundreds more, but suffice to say that by reconditioning our mind (which has little to do with our thinking mind or intuitive mind and so much to do with our feeling mind) we will be reconditioning our results.

A fun way for us to "hear ourselves" and the words we use, is to ask for the assistance of others. Ask those who are around you all the time, such as your family members and employees, to bring to your attention the "limiting" words you use, such as negatives with the action we don't want, as in the example above: *I won't lose my cool.* What you're communicating to your mind and the minds of others is "lose your cool". By enlisting these people on your own personal development support team there's a lot of fun to be had by everyone . . . when your spouse, your children, your employees are permitted by you to hold up the mirror in order to show you when you are making mistakes!

Minimizing Tolerations

One of the most constant obstacles stopping us from receiving the results we most want in our businesses, that will enable us to enjoy the lifestyle we dream of and that seems to elude us, is our very own TOLERATIONS. We tolerate so many things, believing (because we've been programmed to believe this) that "it's not so bad"; "I can put up with that"; "there's nothing I can do about it anyway" and the biggest one, likely is: "I'm just not willing to pay the price."

These myriad items we're tolerating every single day bring us down . . . every single day. We don't even realize what all we're tolerating anymore because they've become ingrained habits.

Habits are actions we take without even realizing we're doing it.
A habit is something we do without thinking.

The simplest way to receive the results we desire . . . as opposed to our current results . . . is to develop habits that serve us better than the ones we currently have. Many people talk about "breaking" habits. It's no wonder, to me, why it's so difficult for us to "break our habits", when we refer back to the section, above, talking about *the Language we Use.* The action "to break" is felt (in our feeling mind, which is 90% of our mind) as painful and is, therefore, a negative or undesirable action. Why, therefore, would we want to break our habits? Instead, I encourage you to

Develop habits that serve you better.

From the mind's perspective, this is so much easier to accomplish. Why? Because you're "developing" something . . . our feeling mind likes that, because it's positive. Also, developing something is in alignment with the Universal Principle / Universal Law of Expansion/Growth. Therefore, by telling yourself and others you are developing better habits you will become successful in doing so much more easily than if you were to tell yourself and others that you are focusing on breaking bad habits.

Simple as that!

Do you see how simple it will be to incorporate these business success strategies into *the way things are done around here?* The way I've helped 1000s of people take to enjoy much greater success in their personal lives . . . **through their businesses** . . . is so simple. Everything I teach is simple. The complication, making it not so easy to implement the changes in *the way things are done around here*, comes from our own internal programming. With proper support, however, helping you to j.f.d.i. and then consistently & persistently *FOLLOW THROUGH*, as you'll learn about in Strategy #3 herein, these simple tactics & strategies will become *easy* to implement.

TURN TO YOUR NOTEBOOK now and list everything you are currently tolerating—everything. I challenge my clients to list a minimum of 27 items and, amazingly, after they get past the 1ˢᵗ 7 the next 20 lines on the page aren't enough. So, it's not necessary to stop at 27 tolerations. It's essential that you continue listing them as you identify them. Only then will you become consciously aware of everything you are tolerating and only then will you eliminate all of these self-imposed obstacles that are keeping you thinking small and holding you back, causing you to feel frustrated, overwhelmed and disillusioned with your current business results. And on that note, there's another e-book you can easily download from Amazon that, again, is a quick and easy read but miles deep with understanding about how we hold ourselves back by thinking so small. I encourage you to study that booklet, as well. It's called **3 Huge Obstacles**

that keep **Small Business Owners feeling Frustrated, Overwhelmed and Disillusioned with their Businesses** and how you, too, can **Overcome Them.**

I recommend you list all of your tolerations in one column, let's say on the left-hand side of the page, and then opposite each toleration commit to one simple action you will take to at least start to eliminate that toleration. You may only be minimizing for the moment, though because you've now written it down in your notebook or binder you will (right?) come back to this list of tolerations and continue to minimize all of them such that they all become eliminated. To help you get started, here are a couple of examples:

Toleration	**Immediate Action to Eliminate Toleration**
Paying suppliers on or after the due-date, causing loss of early-payment bonus and/or late-payment charges	Increase line of operating credit at Bank

Of course, I'm not suggesting you go deeper into debt. I'm recommending you pay less in the way of interest as a first step towards "eliminating" tolerating losing the 2% or 3% early-payment bonus or paying the 2.5%/month (30%/year) late-payment charge. By increasing your Line of Credit you may be paying 6 or 10% and to offset that you'll now receive that 2% early-payment bonus, dramatically bringing your interest charges down. Once you get that in play you would then take another step towards eliminating that toleration and, like Troy, I know that you, too, will be paying your supplier in time to receive the 2% bonus within 4½ months without using your line of credit to do so.

Another example is an equally common occurrence with small businesses:

Toleration	**Immediate Action to Eliminate Toleration**
Receiving phone calls from family and friends during business hours	Ask all personal callers to call me during the evenings or leave a message at home

Cost of Each Interruption

Research has shown that it costs 7 minutes for each and every interruption we have, simply for the interruption: getting off-track from our train of thought; the loss of clarity and motivation with what we were working on; etc. Identify the number of personal calls and even personal e-mails you receive in a day and multiply that number by 7 minutes (not counting the amount of time spent dealing with the call/foolishly reading the forwarded email). Once you determine your own personal hourly worth (not necessarily the rate you charge for your billable time) you'll be shocked at how much money these unimportant interruptions are costing you and your family—and many of them are even caused by your family members.

To help you identify the cost to you, let's say that as an entrepreneur your hourly "worth" is a mere $120 (for ease in doing the math). Now, let's say you permit a mere 10 interruptions each and every day and we all know that the vast majority of the population welcomes far more than just 10 each day. At 7 minutes per interruption, that equates to ($120/60 minutes = $2/minute) 7 minutes per interruption x $2 x 10 interruptions = $140/day

Let's say you do take one 1-month vacation plus 2 1-week vacations and another 2-week vacation each year. That's 52 weeks **minus** 8 for vacations = 44 weeks @ 4 days/week (let's say you do start taking one day off each week for "you" time) = 176 work days x $140/day for interruptions = $24,640.

Now I encourage you to become painfully aware of the number of interruptions you do have in a day and then do the math for yourself. As I say to my clients while I teach them this: If you don't see any value in saving that kind of money for yourself and/or your family, feel free to send it to me at the end of each month and I give them my mailing address. Just think of how much more productive you'll be when you minimize these interruptions, so that you're not just saving $24,640 but you're also giving yourself an additional 70 minutes x 176 days = 12,320 minutes (or 205.33 hours or 25.67 8-hour workdays) each year to implement that many more ideas into your business.

Until you educate all of those people who are barging in on your productive time about these statistics, however, they don't know the consequences of disturbing you during focus time because, after all, you've taught them to do so.

Again, are you seeing how making very *simple* changes to *the way things are done around here* can and will drastically increase your **PROFITS**? And with increased profits and income, do you see that you will be enjoying at least quadruple the **FUN** . . . not only on the more frequent 5-star vacations you'll be enjoying but also during business hours. As for building **RETIREMENT** on your terms, that's simply a by-product of increased profits and enjoying life a lot more because you're finally, truly OPEN to receiving SUCCESS in your business. I repeat:

It's as simple as that!

You've just learned a lot of concepts that you feel are either completely new to you (which I doubt, because as I tell all of my clients: *There's nothing new in business.*) or have a new spin on old concepts. Either way, I understand from my own personal experiences as a small business owner that what I've just shared with you is a lot to digest in a short period. The best way to benefit from the knowledge contained in the previous pages and in the following pages, as well, is to experience the knowledge, becoming aware of how simple it is as well as how resistant you currently are to success. Only by getting out of the river and up onto the bridge I'm offering through this book, then crossing this Bridge of Awareness, which seems to be laden with all types of uncertainties all along the way tempting you to turn back. And as we're just about across the bridge we start to gain awareness. At this point, as the light-bulb comes on for us, which is more like a floodlight, we arrive in the *Land of Understanding*, as I call it. It's in this place where we replace: *I know! I know!* with: **Ahhh. Now I understand.**

BRIDGE of AWARENESS (through **EXPERIENCES**)

Using everything you've just learned or received more clarity on, I'd like to take you back to the items you listed in the categories of things you want to do, things you want to have and who you want to become. I mentioned itemizing at least 7 but you can just as successfully have 17 or 27. (I caution you, however, against overwhelming yourself with "goals".) For each item on the list I encourage you to ask yourself these questions, writing one clear, concise sentence for each answer:

1. Why do I want to _____(do/have/be) this? (If you're unable to answer it with a feeling of passion, excitement or at least pleasure, cross it off your list. It isn't that important after all and likely isn't even *your* desire.)

2. Will _____ing (doing/having/being) this improve the areas of my company or my personal life that I deem important? (If "no" for any item, cross it off your list.)

3. Prioritize the goals you listed earlier that have not been stricken off your list from Questions 1 and 2, above. Write each of the remaining goals on a separate sheet of paper. Answer this question for each one, creating a list of all you can think of: What are the benefits of _____ing (doing/having/being) this to
   - me;
   - my family;
   - my employees;
   - my customers.

   (NOTE: There should be numerous benefits for each of the 4 categories and no fewer than 3.)

4. Working on one goal at-a-time, itemize the steps you need to take to reach that destination. Beside each of the steps, which now become **mini-goals**, indicate whether it's a(n)
   - ongoing goal needing daily input/activity;
   - short-term goal to be achieved between one month and 90 days;
   - medium-term goal that may take between 90 days and a year; and,
   - long-term goal that may take longer than a year.

   [NOTE: I use the word "may" in these sentences because you, too, will be blown away with how many of these goals will simply *appear* without your having to push, struggle, strive, sacrifice or work *hard* on achieving them (work diligently, yes, but not *hard)*.**]**

5. Who needs to know about these goals? Too many employers/managers forget about the role their staff/employees play in getting the company to the level of success the employer wants and dreams of. At a minimum, your goals and your 3-year vision need to be shared with your family **AND** your staff, but not every goal needs to be shared with every person.

    Beside each goal, list the people with whom you need to share that goal to ensure no one is left out-of-the-loop. After all . . .

    a chain is only as strong as its weakest link.

6. Review each goal. Put at least one "action" / step to be taken beside each of the goals.

7. Beside each action step, place a date on or by which you WILL take that step. To give it more power, do this in a different coloured ink. How often have you said "I should . . ." but never "get around to it"?

8. Beside the date on/by which you will take this action step, give the step a "time value." How much time will you need to complete this—to take this step? ½ hour? ½ day? If numerous hours, I recommend you break it into chunks—maybe 1-hour but certainly no longer than 2 hours, because our attention can't last any longer than that—productively, at any rate.

9. Open your calendar—**NOW.** Just set this book down and go get your calendar. It really is this important towards clearing and paving the way for these items to transpire. Now, with your calendar, make at least 3 appointments with yourself to come back to this exercise, for a "chunk" of time in each appointment—remember, no longer than 2 hours each. At those appointments, continue to work through this exercise.

FOR OPTIMUM RESULTS in creating your likely first-ever NTBP (Non-Traditional Business Plan), I encourage you to go on a 3-day retreat. Going on this retreat takes you away . . . away from all of your usual interrupters and distractions and puts you into a different environment; ideally a bigger, nicer, more luxurious environment, one into which you will grow yourself and your business over the next few years. Even just being in this "more" environment will help you stick to the task and encourage you to *get it done*! (May I recommend a place such as Malaga, in the South of Spain? Wow! That one helped me create my best-ever NTBP!)

I know from my own experience and from the experiences of my clients that the difference in the speed and the ease at which you'll reap the rewards of your efforts is like the difference between day and night. In the start of every year-long *Trade-Contractors' Business College* program, as I'm training on Strategy # 1, as I've been covering in this chapter, I explain to the participants in the program, or maybe I warn them, that the sooner they complete their 3-year vision and the stricter they are with themselves in following the steps I lay out for them, for example by going off on a 3-day retreat, the more successful they'll be and the faster and more easily their desires will materialize. Completing the WRAR, which you'll learn about in the chapter explaining Strategy #2, is another indicator of those who will be the most successful throughout this *T-CBC* program. During the years I've delivered this program completing the exercises in Strategies 1 and 2 have proven to be the key indicators to me of who will **SOAR** with their businesses and who will stay in "resistance" and continue to struggle.

NTBP Case Study

> The most powerful story I have seen unfold so far about the ROI on the investment of time & money in creating his NTBP, is that of an electrical contractor who'd been in business for 14 years, had 5 or 6 technicians in the field and had made a decision to finally throw in the towel. By the Grace of God, he wasn't yet a good decision-maker because he didn't take immediate action and when he saw an announcement of a workshop I was leading for his trade's association, he immediately secured his seat at the workshop.

> He not only invested in the year-long-and-deep *Trade-Contractors' Business College* program, but 4 or 5 months into the program he also invested in 1-on-1 weekly coaching with me, which he continued for an entire year, even after having completed the *T-CBC*, before he decided to "take a break from coaching" and continue implementing the various changes we'd been working on. He asked me to contact him again in about 3 months' time when we'd pick up from where we left off, which I did. I heard nothing back from him until some 4 months later, when he called looking for a referral for a recruiter of technical employees. In our conversation he told me that he felt they were right back to where he'd been before he met me: *Flying by the seat of their pants.* He just knew it had to be the quality of the players he was choosing for his

team. I recalled from months earlier that we had worked diligently on this entrepreneur's leadership skills, and I asked him a few pointed questions. We decided to refocus on the essentials like communication, leadership, follow-through, etc. Basically, re-strengthening the foundation of his business. After all, in the 2 years since we'd met his business no longer resembled anything on what he had been throwing in the towel just a short time earlier! They'd never before been where they were at the time of his "urgent" call to me. It stood to reason that without the consistent and persistent support in growing his business his business was struggling again. In fact, we identified that in less than 2 years from having created his first-ever NTBP, his 3-year vision, this entrepreneur had greatly surpassed his vision. He told me that he couldn't even have dreamt 2 years earlier of having the business results he was enjoying today. They hadn't even been in his realm of possibility.

He saw the value of having invested in a 3-day retreat to create his first-ever NTBP—3-year vision—and fewer than 2 months later he went off to create his 2nd-ever NTBP, only this time he could see a lot bigger results and a lot further into the future, so he even sketched in some things for 10 years from then.

And just 2 years from that date, he not only had one of the major components in place for his RETIREMENT, but the other component simply presented itself to him. If he were to do nothing else in the next 8 years but strengthen, improve and grow these 3 combined businesses, this "*lucky*" (as some of his friends are calling him) young entrepreneur could fully retire at the age of 55. As he's now seeing today, however, and as I've known all along, he will do far more in the upcoming 8 years than that. Limits don't exist. With proper support obstacles are quickly and easily removed. Going off half-cocked simply doesn't happen with the constant support of a business coach.

Where would you like to be 3 years from today?

How big can you dream?

How big will you allow yourself to play?

Are you tired of settling for less?

Are you tired of settling for less than this entrepreneur, mentioned above, now enjoys? This, from a man who was throwing in the towel just a very few years ago.

Are you tired of sacrificing your personal and family life for your struggling business?

Are you tired of struggling to achieve the business results you dream of?

Are you ready to take yourself seriously? If so, make a commitment to the exercises in this book and you'll be as amazed as the gentleman above is with how much faster and how much more easily you can grow your business so that you will get to Strategy #7 . . .

> ***GET A LIFE** outside of the business:*
> *DO what you LOVE and LOVE what you DO.*

CHAPTER THREE

Map Out the Route to Reach Your Destination

Strategy # 2
MAP OUT THE ROUTE: Plan Time to Plan Business Developments . . .
and HONOUR it!

"How will my **3-year Vision (my Non-Traditional Business Plan)** ever come to fruition, when I'm so busy putting out fires and dealing with crises every day?" you (like so many others) ask. **By planning, that's how.**

If you've completed the exercises in the previous chapter you now know, more or less, what your business will look like 3 years from today. Now when I say "more or less" I mean that in a very positive light. I have found time–and–again that my 3-year visions materialize in 2 years . . . to the month! A friend, who'd been a client some time ago, said to me in a friends' chat, when I was explaining to her that yet again my very sizeable 3-year vision had come to fruition in just 2 years: *Lynne! No! It's hard enough for me to create a 3-year vision. Don't shorten it to 2 years!* So I haven't. It's still a 3-year vision as you just saw, but like the entrepreneur whose story I just shared with you . . . you, too, can receive your 3-year vision in 2 years' time, or less.

Let's refer to this vision as your destination. How will you get there? Do you know the way? What are the first steps you need to take? And the next steps?

This is precisely why I call Strategy #2 Mapping out the Route, of course. Just like for anywhere you've never been before, when you get behind the wheel you need to have at least an idea of the direction in which to point your vehicle before you put your foot on the gas, right? That's what Strategy #2 is all about. We can call it the "planning" strategy. We hear a lot these days about Strategic Planning. That certainly falls under this heading, that's for sure, but the exercises I'm going to share with you in this chapter are far more than just creating a Strategic Plan for your business. You're now including your personal and family life, as well, and of utmost importance, you're setting yourself up so that **this time** you're going to **follow through**. It's in the next chapter, in fact, that we delve deeply into the *follow-through* component by looking at what's stopped you from following through on many of your goals and desires up to this point, but in this chapter you'll acquire the tools needed to measure your results—much like seeing how many kilometers or miles you've travelled in a certain period, knowing when to refuel, identifying when it's time to pull over and rest, where to eat, where you'll spend the night to recharge your batteries. Wouldn't you agree that these are all very essential components to a successful journey? After all, this isn't a day-trip. Your business is a journey.

I warn you, however, before I present you with all of these user-friendly tools that will have you mapping out the route to your destination, that your biggest challenge in making these tools work will be to

Honour the Planning.

Of course, as I mentioned, focus on the *follow-through* will be in the next chapter, though I want to stop you now from paying any attention whatsoever to that negative voice inside that's going to tell you, as you read through this and work on the exercises, that you already know this and you've already *been there; done that* and it didn't work then so it won't work now. This is an example of our feeling mind's vocabulary, which you would think would be working *with* us, not *against* us, however, this is our programming. That kind of inner talk keeps us small and keeps us from taking risks. Therefore, as you're reading the following pages and working through the exercises, I remind you to remain *open-minded* and open to the possibility (like Lionel found does exist, which you can hear at **www.mljcoaching.com/testimonials/**) that you can actually enjoy all those goals you currently long to achieve.

Segmenting our Days

I was first introduced to this by my first coaching mentor, Chris Barrow, and I instantly saw the accuracy and simplicity of first segmenting our days in order to compartmentalize the tasks we assign to the hours in these days.

Let's imagine that we are only allowed to have three types of days in our lives:

Free Days   **Focus Days**   **Buffer Days**

Free Day = day off

These are the days on which you rest, recuperate, recharge your batteries and reconnect with yourself and with the people who truly matter to you outside of work. They're days when you fulfill your roles as a 'self', a family member, a friend, etc. Allow your very capable team to address any and all work-related items that arise. If your team isn't available because they're all off for the weekend or for any other reason, teach your customers that your personal time is very valuable to you (as theirs can be to them). On **free** days you're not even reading this book, doing these exercises or any other further education, nor popping into the office, checking e-mails, doing the business newsletter or the books on the laptop on the kitchen table. Your cell phone is turned off! Maybe, like Jim, Sylvio & numerous others, you need to buy yourself a personal cell phone, giving the new number only to family & friends. There is no work in your vehicle that would cause you angst when you get into the vehicle to go somewhere to have **FUN**!

It's important that you understand that your FREE DAYs are not only vacation days, but they also include your days off in each week. They aren't necessarily the weekends, but I do *strongly recommend* that you take 2 **full** days off each week—together, back-to-back. When you absolutely must work late, I recommend you do it in the evening of a workday, as opposed to the morning of a day-off.

Free Days must be complete days—not partial days, otherwise they're only "free" hours.

Focus Day = focused on getting results

These are the days when you're concentrating on doing whatever it is you do for which you get paid; whatever brings money into your business or directly causes money to come into your business. You're leading your team (staff/employees), communicating with customers, selling your product, networking, getting referrals. You're focused on results—and sticking to your 3 MIAs: *Most Important Activities*. It's time for you to become very strict with your time. You will no longer allow *the freedom of being my own boss* interruptions—like spur-of-the-moment family duties, chatting with friends who pop in to visit when you're focused on growing your business, speaking with sales people who drop in unexpectedly and unannounced on their monthly rounds, and whatever other types of interruptions you invite into your FOCUS time to take and keep you off-track and struggling to get the results you just *know* your business could be enjoying—*if only* . . . .

To help you become very clear on the activities on which you *should* be focusing during these FOCUS days, let's identify what *your* MIAs are. Experience has shown me that regardless of which industry we're in or the size of our businesses these MIAs are something like:

1. Delivering to your customers (if you're at least a somewhat established business)
2. Sales (which may include marketing) (and growing your contacts list if you have no existing customer database to draw from—more in Strategy #6)
3. Leading your team (and as you'll see in Strategy #5, everyone has a support team, even if they're unpaid)

Note: In the event that you don't yet have customers, or something has happened to cause your business to be in such a state that you currently have no or very few customers, your 1st priority, your Most Important Activity, will be **SALES**. Why? Because . . .

without sales you don't have a business.

Simple as that!

For every activity I encourage you to block chunks of time into your agenda. For example:

7 - 7:15	Study, Reflection & Daily Planning
7:15 - 7:30	Review messages and prioritize activities
7:30 - 7:45	Meet with team regarding day's production
7:45 - 8	Return calls and respond to e-mails
8 - 8:15	Meet with Administration Manager
8:15 - 9:30	**Business Development Time**
9:30 - 9:35	Stretch your legs and collect messages from Admin Manager
9:35 - 11	Estimating/Creating Proposals
11 - noon	Site visit(s)

Noon - 1 pm   Lunch with _(insert name of 'A' Customer)_

1 - 1:30   Return calls; check in with Admin Manager

1:30 - 3   On-site training with _(insert name of employee)_

3 - 4   Return to office and respond to crucial messages/e-mails

4 - 4:15   Fine-tune scheduling for tomorrow

4:15 - 4:30   Fine-tune your 'to-do' list

This is, obviously, a very rough idea of what a daily schedule *could* look like. Some items such as the first few in the morning would be there every day. Others, such as estimating jobs, writing proposals, etc. may occur just 2-3 times each week. If you're spending more time than that on writing proposals or bidding on contracts, it's time to hire an Estimator/Project Manager.

Lunch with 'A' customers may only occur once each week, depending on the necessity for boosting your in-flow of cash (in which case you'll have up to 5 'A' customer luncheons each week as you'll learn more about in the chapter focusing on Strategy #6). Once each week you could spend up to ½-hour or so to prepare the week's schedule for your team, if you do this in your business. There will be monthly meetings, such as your MMM (Monthly Management Meeting, which you'll learn about shortly), your safety training, etc. that will take 2 hours, but happen just once each month.

I can't even tell you what I do with my days! I feel so frustrated at the end of the day, feeling I haven't accomplished anything.

As you can imagine, I hear words to this effect very frequently. To determine what all needs to go into your daily planner you need to identify what you spend your time on each day . . . for an entire month. It's really very simple to do. Carry a pocket-sized/purse-sized notebook with you, along with a pen and keep it open in your vehicle as you travel around as well as on your desk with you in the office. Simply write down absolutely everything you do from start to finish of your days. Only a 1-or-2-word description is required for each task and the time-of-day that you start the task. It will go without saying that the amount of time you spent on that task is identified by the start-time of the following task. Yes, this sounds like a pain, I know. However, short-term pain for long-term gain pays huge dividends in the end. The secondary use of this fact-finding task is that as you identify what all you spend your valuable time on each day you will be able to block appropriate chunks of time into your agenda *and* you'll identify which tasks you can delegate to people on your team.

Buffer Day = all the other stuff associated with being in business

This is the day when you deal with all the other 'stuff'—administration, government "stuff", business and technical reading, continuing education, recruiting & hiring (unless your business is growing very quickly and you're constantly hiring, in which case this will be in your FOCUS time), fixing shelves, reorganizing your physical environment, business/personal budgets (because they're only created once each year), correspondence, research, etc. In a nutshell, your buffer time is for those activities you don't do frequently; otherwise they're in your agenda during your FOCUS time. How much buffer time or how many buffer days do you need per month to keep the business rolling? Typically half a day per month should be ample, but you may require more time in getting started while you clean up the back-log.

After you've assigned everything you can from this list to your team, explain to them that you are not to be disturbed because you need to concentrate. Because activities in your **Buffer** category appear to everyone else to be of very low priority, you're apt to receive many interruptions because you actually welcome them (otherwise you would never be interrupted). Communicate the importance of your buffer time and these buffer activities to your team. Close the door. Turn off your phone. The less time you, yourself, spend on these non-billable activities, that are essential house-keeping for your business, the better. Nonetheless, there isn't a business out there without lower-priority activities that simply will become higher priorities if neglected. By dealing with these lower priorities before they flare up to a high priority, jamming a cog in the wheel, they will be dealt with much faster and much more easily because they'll be dealt with calmly and without stress.

Strategic Planning—from 1-year all the way down to a Daily 'to-do' list

In our 3-day 3-year vision retreats it's simple to simply extract our **1-year plan**, which includes goals to reach during the 1st 1-year period of our 3-year vision, right? These goals will, of course, cover each of the various categories, such as business, finance, family, friends/social, etc. which you included in your 3-year vision. Otherwise, how can you ever expect to reach your destination (your 3-year vision) for your business if you're totally neglecting your physical health, your family obligations, your social and family fun, as well as your family's financial health and wealth? From our 1-year plan it's easy to extract our 1st set of 90-day goals which, again, include all of those various categories you used in your 3-year vision and 1-year plan. *Sound simple?*

During your 3 other **90-day goal-setting/Strategic Planning** meetings throughout the year I recommend you set aside at least ½-day in your agenda around the middle of the month. The reason I say mid-month is so that you'll be sure to have your monthly Profit & Loss statements from the most recent month to take with you on this ½-day retreat.

To ensure we're on-track towards reaching our 90-day goals, rather than having the 90-day period sneak up on us and we've forgotten what we'd even set as goals (can you tell this happens regularly with numerous small business owners?), again *it's very simple.* We have **monthly "management" meetings (MMM)** with our key people, key person or even just by yourself if you're running a very small operation or with your spouse, if (s)he's your sounding board, cheerleader and/or accountability partner. For these meetings, at a minimum, you're reviewing your Profit & Loss statements from the previous month and comparing them to your financial projections for the year, you're reviewing your cash-flow situation, you're reviewing the minutes of the previous meeting with your management team to ensure all of the actions from that meeting have been taken, you're analyzing the sales reports, you're grading your customers (A, B & C), reviewing your many marketing tactics such as added-value, newsletter, referral, networking, etc. This is also a crucial time for you to review the team's performance, individual's development, training, etc. Many small businesses owned in partnership conduct meetings such as this, but it always surprises me to see how many don't. The partners know they "should" be conducting these meetings, but trust that *if anything serious were to come up we'd deal with it.*

Whether you're in the partnership-owned business not having these monthly management meetings or you're a sole proprietor who doesn't see the necessity, please heed my warning:

Small businesses that do not behave like professional businesses will always be amateurs.

Just look at the difference in profit between a professional athlete or entertainer and an amateur. Which would you rather be?

Yes, meetings take time. This can be one of the biggest wastes of time in any business—even if you're the sole-proprietor meeting with yourself to review all of these categories. Because I believe that TIME is the ONLY limited resource, I also believe it's imperative that for every activity you perform you block time into your agenda for the activity.

Similar to my recommendation of 3 days for your 3-year vision, at least 1 day for your 1-year planning (where you review your 3-year vision and expand it to bring it back up to a 3-year vision now that a year has passed) and at least ½-day retreats for your 90-day goals, I recommend a maximum of 2 hours for your MMM (Monthly Management Meetings). A very fun-loving, dynamic "larger" small-business under the helm of 5 partners with whom I've had the pleasure of being a partner to enhance their business comes to mind, and before our partnership their MMMs (Monthly Management Meetings) were taking all evening long. Some partners would show up late, with the rest sitting there waiting, agitated from a stressful day. They would become very animated at times and routinely went way off-track with the frustrations and passion of each and every one of them. By the end of these long meetings they didn't even feel as though they'd accomplished much, but out of energy and out of time they had to promise to resume the discussion later.

Especially for meetings with others, and even with yourself, it's essential to have a clearly itemized list of business to discuss and a value of time, ie. 5, 10, 15 etc. minutes per topic. Any action to be taken is written down and for group meetings (even groups of 2) the Minutes of the Meeting are printed, with the action, completed 'by when' and 'by whom', and distributed. All action, unless otherwise stated, ought to be completed inside of 1 week, otherwise you risk the action never being taken.

Include STUDY in your Daily Strategic Planning

You may have noticed in my example of a daily schedule under FOCUS time, that I included 15 minutes at the start of each day for your *daily* strategic planning. I used to say that this could be done either at the end of the day or the beginning of the day, because it also included fine-tuning your 'to-do' list, which you see I've scheduled for the end of each day. I now know better than to suggest doing your Daily Planning at the end of the day and this is why I have broken these tasks into the last and first 15 minutes of the day. These pillars of time support each day of your business, holding the space for you to switch ON and switch OFF every single day.

Included in your reflective planning time, which really must be at the beginning of each day, I now recommend that you include study. Typically, I would recommend you study personal development material in that time (as opposed to studying tactical or technical material, such as what's contained in this book or industry training). In fact a book I highly recommend you study for the first few minutes of each morning for the rest of your business life is *Think and Grow Rich*, by Napoleon Hill (and do be sure to find "the original" as I see there are many versions now available). And even simpler yet is a video you can download from Youtube called *The*

Strangest Secret, by Earl Nightingale. That's even simpler to study than a book, because it's an audio that you can put onto your smart phone and listen to everywhere. There are numerous fabulous books to study which will help you in your own personal development, and once you've been through *Think and Grow Rich* a couple or few times it would be my pleasure to recommend more great works along these lines. Know you are always welcomed to contact me through **info@mljcoaching.com**.

The reason I recommend personal development study for small business owners is because

your business can only ever become as big as you are.

If you want your business to grow, you must first lead the way. By studying for a few brief moments each day your personal development will expand and so will your business. Without it, as I say, your business simply can't grow any bigger. It's an amazing fact and I see it in action on a daily basis.

You may find it easier to complete the first task of your day, as suggested above, at home, if you have solitude there first thing in the morning, if even on your front deck. Otherwise, if you arrive to a quiet office for a good 15-20 minutes, that would be an ideal place to study, reflect and plan for the day ahead. If not, you may need to do this in your vehicle.

The way I study on a daily basis, as I say, is by having a 15-minute chunk of time blocked out. I start by reading where I left off the previous day in one of my fabulous personal development books, such as *Think and Grow Rich* which I've already read and studied through some 6-7 times and which is always with me regardless of in which continent, country, province, state or city I find myself. In fact, I now have the habit of picking up this book, in particular, before I start a VIP Intensive coaching session with a client. Instead of picking up where I left off, I allow the book to fall open to any page it chooses. I then read what's on that page until I have an understanding of what's there—and typically, it's only one page. I now know that this is what my client needs my help to focus on the most; and sure enough: It's spot on every time. Once I've greeted the client, and we've gone through some chit-chat and formalities about how the session will unfold we dive right in with my usual asking of:

How can I help you?

It may take an hour or 3 but we always get around to what's deeply holding the client back and *BINGO!* That's when I recall what I had studied just before we started our VIP Intensive session. Sure enough, it's precisely what the client needed, but until it came into context it would have been impossible for me to explain in a way the client could grasp its application to his/her situation. This is why I feel that Napoleon Hill's *Think and Grow Rich* is the best book for you to start with in your daily study, reflection and planning.

As I read from where I left off in the book I'm studying at that time, I only read as many lines, paragraphs or pages as it takes until I find myself reflecting on a passage—thinking about an example in my life that relates to what I just read. This seldom takes me onto the 3rd page, even and oftentimes it's after only 2 or 3 paragraphs. As I find myself reflecting, I close the book. I continue to reflect on how what I've just read applies to my situation, whether in business or my personal life or a client's situation, even. Once my mind has wandered off from that on which I was reflecting, I simply ask myself:

What are my 3 HHWs for today?

HHWs is a name one of my clients lovingly gave the purpose of his WRAR, which you'll learn about momentarily. HHW stands for Hell or High Water. Once my reflection has ended, I ask myself: "Come hell or high water today, what are the 3 most important tasks that must be completed?" And my mind, being conditioned/programmed like everyone else's, dutifully answers the question . . . and so will yours. Again: *It's as simple as that!* Therefore, on a daily basis, in just 15 minutes you will have enhanced your ability to focus on what you want (as opposed to what you don't) and you will have identified the 3 major tasks that, come hell or high water, you will ensure be completed before the day is done and I recommend you do them first. Then, should a fabulous opportunity come along you are free to seize it. Or, if you're feeling frustrated, exhausted, overwhelmed or disillusioned like most small business owners when we first meet, after these 3 HHWs are completed: Take the rest of the day off. Go golfing. Go fishing. Go take a nap. Whatever your 'self' needs most at this moment, gift it to you. Once you're back to feeling charged again in your business, once your 3 daily HHWs are completed, you'll be in good stead to start knocking off some of those B or C priorities.

The importance of working from a list of just 3 items can't be stressed enough. One client, working with me in a year-long group training & coaching program, after having already worked with me in the VIP Intensive program before that, was again feeling frustrated, becoming overwhelmed as his business had gone from not having enough work for next month to now trying to fit smaller projects in and around the 3-year projects that seemed to have come to them from out-of-the-blue. I asked about his daily HHWs. Oh, yes, he assured me, he had his to-do list in front of him every day all day long. It was like his bible, he told me. As we dug deeper I helped him understand the importance of working from this HHW list that contains *only 3 items*. As he completed those 3 HHWs he could then refer back to his 20-item to-do list and bring another 3 to the top and put them onto a separate list—containing only 3 items. Two weeks later we discussed again how he was feeling and he sheepishly admitted, more to himself than to me, that all these months he had been so resistant to use a separate sheet of paper to create a new list of 3 items because it just seemed silly. He couldn't see the difference it could possibly make . . . until he did it, because he was at a loss for anything he could see that would work better to relieve him of this new overwhelming feeling. By having only 3 items on your list you feel accomplished once you've completed them, causing you to feel accomplished 2, 3, 4 times each day (rather than overwhelmed or frustrated) as you continue to short-list your 20+ items. Alternatively, as he was leaving the office late each day he would review these 20+ items with some of them not yet stricken off, feeling frustrated because he didn't accomplish everything that day.

Therein lies the importance of listing only 3 items at-a-time. Conduct an experiment for yourself with this. Pay close attention to how you feel at the end of the day looking at a never-ending to-do list, compared to how you feel at day's-end reviewing all of your completed 3-item lists.

"So where do these HHWs fit into my agenda?" you may be wondering.

As you've identified what it is you do all day by keeping track in your pocket—or purse-sized agenda, you've delegated many of those little tasks that others can do *lots well enough* and you've categorized the rest. Remember your 3 MIAs?

Link everything you do . . . everything . . . to your goals.

If you're investing time on activities that are not getting you closer to your 90-day goals, hence your 1-year plan and 3-year vision, then the activities on which you're spending valuable time and energy are taking you farther away. *Simple, right?* Yet so many of us spend so much of our time on activities that either don't need to be done by us or don't even need to be done at all. This means that the majority of one's time is spent *taking them away from their goals.* Is it any wonder you struggle to reach the business success you just know you should be enjoying?

Therefore, simply chunk time into your agenda for those tasks that fit into your 3 MIA categories; which, naturally, take you closer to your 90-day goals . . . which, of course, take you closer to your 1-year plan and your 3-year vision.

Your HHWs, in answer to the question above, fit into categories towards

- Delivering services and/or products to your clients;
- Sales (and marketing for future sales);
- Leading your team;

which are activities such as strengthening relationships with your "top" clients, if your team are the ones who actually deliver the services and/or products. If you, like I, deliver the services to your clients and contribute greatly to creating the programs and products, then you will need chunks of "client" time in your agenda. If this is the case for you, as it is for me, I recommend that you serve all of your clients more-or-less back-to-back. For example, as I write this book, my "client" days are all-day Mondays and 2/3 of Tuesdays. If you spread your clients out all over the week, you'll find it much more difficult to block other activities that take sizeable chunks of time, such as attending networking meetings, creating marketing campaigns, business development, etc.

Likewise, when it comes to leading your team it's imperative that you meet with the 1-3 key people on your team *daily*, if only for 5-10 minutes. Then weekly you'll want to have lengthy meetings with the key person for each department, such as your Administrative Manager, your Project Management Manager, your Comptroller. For each of these weekly meetings, regardless of their length, you want to have a Meeting Agenda, which will help keep all or both of you on task, followed by Minutes of the Meeting distributed within 48 hours.

We've now got the structure pretty well covered for completing your agenda. However, the "*sticking to it*" will be covered in Strategy #3 and, of course, is up to you. I've explained how simple it is to break your 3-year vision into chunks, right down to daily chunks to put into your agenda. There is one more beneficial document for you to complete . . . on a weekly basis. You've got your 3-year vision, your 1-year plan, your 90-day goals which you review during your Monthly Management Meetings and arguably the 2nd most critical document, 2nd to your 3-year vision, is your **WRAR**—*Weekly Reflection and Achievements Review* form. This document, which is included at the end of this chapter for your replication, is completed once each week during your Business Development time. You'll see how simple the questions are and by answering those same questions every single week for a year, you will successfully reach all 4 sets of your 90-day goals. In turn, you'll also follow your 1-year plan, and you'll have your year documented, much like a journal, so that you can look back and remind yourself of how daunting the challenge to implement this structure into your business felt while you were first reading it—like right now—and this will be proof, as you continue to triple your business results, of how simple it is to do.

I know from the beginning of a program more-or-less who will lead the pack, right down to who will get the least benefit out of the program. How? By the dedication they make to completing their WRARs. It's simply a commitment and if you develop the habit of honouring your commitments, especially those you make to yourself, you will see much better results all around—in your business and in your *life outside of the business* (Strategy #7). As you'll see, it's a very simple document. All it takes is your commitment and some 15 minutes each week.

Dispelling the Time–Management Myth

I am continually amazed to hear the words "Time" and "Management" together in a compound word. Do you honestly believe you can manage time? Those seconds, minutes and hours tick by regardless of what we do in them. There's no such thing as time-management. What we can do, however, to receive better results is ***prioritize our activities***. We all have 24 hours in every day—in every continent in the world. You choose to spend your time on certain activities. *Are those the activities which will give you the best results?*

One of the most useful tools I share with my clients is this **Quadrants of Time** which I learned many years ago from one of Stephen Covey's works: *First Things First*. It's absolutely brilliant and if you pay close attention to the quadrant(s) in which you find yourself operating most frequently it could be a business-saver for you, as well as a marriage-saver. Really drilling down to what you spend your time doing, and prioritizing your activities, is the difference between being

- busy, busy, busy and
- focused, occupied and wealthy.

Quadrants of Time

Description of Activities on which you spend your time:

Q1 Urgent <u>and</u> Important	Q3 Urgent . . . but <u>not</u> important
Q2 Not Urgent, but Important	Q4 Neither Urgent <u>nor</u> Important

I suggest you take a few minutes without reading on and study the table above. Before you allow me to teach you about these Quadrants, I'd like you to reflect on them for a moment and see if you can come up with some examples for each of the quadrants and then identify the approximate percentage of time you spend in each of these quadrants.

If I recall correctly, Stephen Covey found that about 80% of the population spends about 80% of their time in **Quadrant 3**—on activities that were URGENT but NOT important. In my years of specializing in working with entrepreneurs in the construction industry, I've found that about 80% of construction contractors spend about 80% of their time in **Quadrant 1**, on activities that are URGENT and IMPORTANT. Ideally, we'll all develop the habit of spending 80% of our time in Q2, focusing on activities that are IMPORTANT and NOT urgent.

Have you arrived at some examples of tasks you do which fit into each of the Quadrants? In which quadrant would you say you currently spend 80% of your time?

Let's start with Stephen Covey's findings. The majority of people, he finds, spend some 80% of their time doing things that are not important but they're urgent—in **Quadrant 3**. How can something that isn't even important be urgent? One of the best examples I have found to paint a picture of this is reading a flyer that comes in the mail or with your newspaper, showing you all of this week's sales. Apparently the Canadian Tire flyer, distributed in Canada (obviously!), is the most-read publication . . . *throughout the entire country*! Many men have admitted to me that they notice if they don't receive their weekly flyer. What's so important about this flyer? "It has a lot of great deals in it. Eventually everything comes on sale at Canadian Tire. You can save a lot of money by spending a few minutes each week looking at the specials."

If you own a business and you need tools or supplies for your business and you wait for them to come on sale, you're wasting time and energy making do without whatever it is you need. Secondly, while the quality may be reasonably good for the price, is this the quality of your business—department-store quality? Furthermore, once you've read that flyer, even if it is during your personal entertainment time, you are now spending gas & vehicle maintenance . . . as well as TIME . . . driving all the way across town before the sale ends to save a few dollars. And, inevitably, you go in for something that's on sale for $9.99 which you feel you need and come out with bags full to the tune of $99.99 of many things you'll likely never even use. How much money did you save, especially after the time we just identified that you wasted by "making do without"? And I haven't even factored in the time spent shopping!

Another great example of Q3 activities is answering your cell phone. Just think about it. More than 80% of the time those calls are unsolicited by you so it's highly unlikely that they're important . . . to you. They're urgent though, because this tool in your belt is either vibrating or making an intrusive noise, and you've been trained to silence or calm this tool, so you answer it. Again, more than 80% of the time on these unsolicited calls you spend many more minutes than is necessary to deal with this issue which, ultimately, is not even important to you or the success of your business. Many a business owner I've worked with has acquired a new cell phone, with a number given out to a very short list, and handed his/her original phone or SIM card with the phone number over to an employee. The customers' calls are being answered, their issues are being successfully resolved, personal and frivolous calls come to an end when these people aren't reaching you on their whim and **you** are now focusing on Q2 activities.

Quadrant 4 is a ridiculous waste—investing your valuable time in an activity that's neither important nor urgent. One great example of this is surfing the internet. Another is channel surfing on the television. I honestly don't know how entrepreneurs whose businesses are not providing them with absolutely everything their heart desires can allow themselves to spend time in front of mindless television. If you've made a decision to sit down and watch television then I recommend that it be, like in your business agenda, scheduled into your personal agenda. For example, if a worthwhile movie, a sports match, entertaining sitcom or educational program is on at 8 pm on Wednesday evening which you feel is important to watch for family time (again I question TV for this) or personal entertainment, I would recommend you put that onto your kitchen calendar and go to the T.V. room at 7:59 p.m. on Wednesday. Enjoy your program.

Instead, a number of small business owners, when we first start working together, tell me they go to the T.V. room to unwind, relax, de-stress and after channel surfing for an hour or so fall asleep on the sofa. They get just enough sleep there to ruin their night's sleep in bed.

I encourage you to *live life on purpose*. Become very focused and diligent in everything you do. Sleep well; entertain well; enjoy being entertained; work well; be a patient, loving and attentive parent; be a generously giving life partner; etc. Simply put:

Live life on purpose.

As I indicated, **Quadrant 1**, putting out fires, is where most entrepreneurs in the construction industry find themselves . . . and they don't know how to get out. You, too, even though you're in a different industry may find yourself here much too frequently for your liking. Do you remember a game that was around some 40 years ago? It may even be around today. It was called *Whack a Mole.* When you whacked a mole on the head with a wooden hammer more moles would pop up in other places on the board. The object of the game was to get all the moles whacked down into the holes without any others popping back up. This is the image that comes to mind for me to describe Quadrant 1 to you. You no sooner get one fire put out but another fire starts over there and another on the other side of town, etc. Why are these fires starting, anyway? Because your team hasn't been properly trained to do the work well? Because your customers don't know what your agreement regarding the scope of work was? Because supplies and equipment aren't being ordered in advance? Or aren't being delivered as promised? You see, last-minute things come up due to lack of planning.

More often than not, you'll find that your current activities in Quadrant 1 are important, but the **urgency** isn't yours—it's your customers' or your employees' or your service providers' or your family members'. In most instances you have trained all of these people to leave things to the last minute because you tolerate it . . . and because you'll resolve their issues . . . at the last minute. It may be that they used to present their issues to you in advance, and you waited until the last minute to resolve them, anyway. You see, that's currently *the way things are done around here*, in your business. There are simple steps to take to get yourself out of Q1 and they're much easier to take than you think. First and foremost, invest time—in Q2—to identify the systems you want implemented to deal with the various types of activities you're currently dealing with as fires. 2ndly, communicate *the way things are going to be done around here from now on* to everyone who needs to know about them.

To start with, over the next month keep track of all of the **urgent & important** activities that arise. Identify if it really was important, and if so, identify how each of those incidents *could have been* avoided. *Simple as that!* Becoming clear, creating new systems and **communicating** is all it takes.

There are some legitimate incidents that occur, however, that do and will continue to fit into Q1. Let's say you were to unexpectedly cross paths with an old friend from high school who's only in town today and you'd just love to take a couple of hours to get caught up over lunch. To me, that's an example of an important and urgent matter that I would just love to be able to deal with without causing a lot of stress for everyone else on my team. Another example of a Q1 activity could be that your child's school calls and says your little girl was just bitten by a mouse and since they feel she needs to be checked for rabies she needs to go the hospital immediately; or likewise, when she loses consciousness in some type of seizure while at the babysitter's. It never crossed my mind not to go immediately to collect her and take her to the hospital in the city in both of those incidents. Thanks to my work habits it took fewer than 5 minutes to explain what needed to be done during my absence and my sudden exodus caused minimal stress for others.

Spending 80% of your time in **Quadrant 2** is what allows you the freedom to be in Q1 on occasion without putting everyone else into a panic. Quadrant 2 is where you're honouring your agenda that we discussed earlier in this chapter. You have chunks of time for all of the activities which *you* truly must do (remember: the other tasks and activities you have delegated to others) blocked off in your agenda and when those times come up in your agenda you honour them. You make sure you stop responding to e-mails and returning phone calls when your time is up because it's now time to have that meeting with your Administrative Assistant or Administration Manager to ensure you're both brought up-to-speed for the day and for the week ahead, as well as the major projects you're both working on. You make sure your lunch with your 'A' customer doesn't run over because you have calls to return, maybe some you didn't get to in the morning before your meeting with your Admin Manager. You become very strict with yourself and with your agenda. By spending 80% of your time following through on your planning you'll find that there are very few Q1 fires. By ensuring you invest the time to create really good contracts which simply are signed for each job you do, you won't have customers calling you to find out why some part of the job wasn't done, which you didn't feel your company was hired to do. By training your employees systematically, habitually, routinely, they won't be making the mistakes that cause the problems. By communicating clearly with your team they'll all clearly understand what their roles and duties are and they'll perform them to the best of their ability.

Simply by eliminating time currently spent in Q4, minimizing time in Q3 and investing 80% of your time in Q2 you'll relieve so much of the stress you're feeling so that when a Q1 comes up you'll be able to deal with it calmly and effectively. While working diligently in Q2 you are about 80% more productive with your time because you're not under stress to get the job done and you now have no distractions. You're doing the job accurately because you're calm and thinking clearly. You're being pro-active in Q2 as opposed to re-active, which is the mode you're in when you're operating in Q1.

In which Quadrant would you *prefer* to spend the majority of your time?

In the table, below, enter some of your ideal tasks which you would like to see happening in each of these boxes. It's perfectly acceptable to write nothing in Q4 . . . and even Q3 for that matter. Continue the list in your notebook or binder, though I do encourage you to enter some in here as a reminder for every time you're re-working these exercises.

Q1 Urgent <u>and</u> Important, such as _____ _____ _____	Q3 Urgent . . . but <u>not</u> important _____ _____ _____
Q2 Not Urgent, but Important _____ _____ _____	Q4 Neither Urgent <u>nor</u> Important _____ _____ _____

Change doesn't happen overnight, but I guarantee that if you invest 80% of your time and energy to develop habits that serve you well, you will enjoy

a huge increase in **FUN** and **PROFITS**
and a huge decrease in stress and frustration.

Quarterly ½-1-day Retreat

It's critical to go off-site for at least the better part of a day in order to think and plan strategically for the quarter ahead. Get away from your home; get away from the office and have that one-day retreat. If you feel you can't invest an entire day in these quarterly retreats take at least a good ½-day . . . but not first thing in the morning, coming back to work once you've finished, or

---

you'll find yourself rushing to get it done and before you've even really started you're packing up and *getting back to work*. Therefore, if you must take only ½-day, attend to whatever seems so urgent and important (Q1, right?) that it can't wait until the next day or be done by one of your capable employees, then head off on your retreat before lunch. A great way to start a retreat is by breaking bread. The most important meetings in the world include food . . . and the way I see it there's no meeting in your business that's any more important than your Strategic Planning meetings, even if they're only with yourself. The best Business Development meetings for small business owners, I find, are attended by only the business owner. However, if flying solo isn't for you just yet, take along key employee(s) or senior team member(s). I recommend your spouse accompany you **only if (s)he is directly involved in the business.** You definitely want to have a meeting with your spouse/life-partner about the type of lifestyle (s)he would like to enjoy through the business' profits and certainly you'll have this meeting once you return from your 3-day 3-year-vision retreat, but since your lifestyle will up-level *thanks to your improved and increased business results*, it's essential that only the business owner/operator attend this meeting. I'd be delighted to speak to your spouse about this to help her/him understand that it truly is scary for them and limiting for you, otherwise.

Annual Retreat

After your 1st 3-year vision, take 1–2 days out once a year—preferably in your off-season or your season of personal preference—to sort out in your own mind what you're going to do during the following year. (See Strategy 1—Construct a Powerful 3-year Vision)

BLOCK TIME instead of Waiting to "Find" it

By this time I'm sure your mind is reeling with the same challenges many entrepreneurs share with me. They have such difficulties "finding" time to get away . . . even if it is in order to implement the new strategies and tactics that they're learning. My response to them is my response to those worries racing around in your mind right now: **Time isn't lost.** Nor does it hide. The vocabulary is just silly that we use when offering up excuses to our families, employees and others when we say

"I'd really like to, but I just can't find the time."

Time is right there in front of our faces every day all day long. You see it ticking by on the wall, on a watch on your wrist, on the screen of your computer, on your "smart" phone and myriad other places such as on your stove, microwave & even your television. So why do we keep trying to "find" it?

Therefore, rather than "looking" for the time, simply block it off in your agenda, commit to it and simply make happen whichever activities you choose to put into your agenda. I know for a fact that you are a much more powerful entrepreneur, parent, life-partner, employer than you think. When you make a decision things happen. If that weren't the case you would never have gotten to where your business is today. It's time to get back to making decisions—quickly—and taking action on them **immediately**. You will find, as you practice doing this, that your business will turn completely around . . . quickly and almost effortlessly.

In order to develop the habit of consistently & persistently creating 90-day goals and 1-year plans, updating your 3-year vision annually, you simply need to book those days off right now. Go ahead and open your agenda right now and books those days in:

- 3 days for your first-ever 3-year vision;
- 2 days at the same time each year from here on in; and
- a good ½-day starting at 11 am or earlier every 90 days as of 90 days from completion of your first-ever 3-year vision.

People usually start by taking a long weekend to work on their 3-year vision, but before the end of the first year they're seeing how this is NOT playing hooky from work. It's actually being probably the most productive they've ever been while working—working on the future and sustainability of their business. Once they understand this they take those ½-day, 1-2-day and even 3-day retreats mid-week, allowing themselves the weekends to play with their families.

Therefore, your exercise now is to open your agenda and commit right now to the dates of your next 3 quarterly ½-day or even 1-day 90-day-goal-setting retreats.

What will you do during these retreats?

Even during the ½-day 90-day-goal-setting retreat, you're getting away from your usual environment—home, office, business—so that you will free yourself from all distractions. During this time, in a nutshell, you'll be deciding: *"**Who will do what and when?**"*

The following is an agenda for these Business Meetings which I've included to help you stay focused, on track and on time.

Step 1   Review your 3-year vision and update it.

Step 2   Review your Professional and Personal Mission Statements and update them.

Step 3   Review your Roles and Goals for each Role you play . . . and update, if necessary (like how I needed to update mine immediately after a Trade-Contractors' Business College workshop gathering, when I went to visit my daughters and learned I was going to become a grandmother—twice over! I needed to update my roles and I sure did!).

Step 4   Colour code your diary for the following year into Free, Focus and Buffer days (in that order).

Step 5   Prepare budgets for personal and business expenditures to create your 'perfect' life financially (See Strategy 4).

Step 6   Ask yourself 'What has to happen for this to happen?'

Step 7   Create your 90-day goals, checking to be sure that they're addressing the answer to the Question in Step 6.

And in answer to a client's question, packing for his first-ever 3-day retreat, here's a list of just some of the items I suggest you take with you. Feel free to take everything else that comes to mind.

There are no hard and fast rules, but I suggest the following:

1. last year's financial records;
2. year-to-date (ie. this year's financial records up to the end of the day you pack for your retreat);
3. last year's calendar (assuming you have your family events and vacations noted therein);
4. this year's calendar;
5. a calendar for next year (which can be printed from Microsoft Outlook or the internet);
6. a couple of magazines to which you subscribe or which you pick up somewhere. For one it may be car racing magazines; for another exotic destinations . . . something that interests you (for me it might be alpine skiing);

7. several pens, pencils, eraser, high-lighters, a few notebooks, scissors, tape, calculator, a sheet of bristol board;

8. a plastic yearly wall planner and whiteboard markers (you can get them at Staples);

9. all unread reading material pertaining to your business;

10. my archived newsletters, in print **http://mljcoaching.com/newsletter-archives**;

11. snacks (so you won't have to leave the room so often to eat);

12. motivational reading material (like *Think & Grow Rich*);

13. information about the current situation for each of the portions of your life (as in Strategy #1);

14. a w—i—d—e opened mind (you are the only limitation to your having, doing and being anything you want to have, do or be);

15. . . . I'll fill you in if/when something more strikes me . . .

REMEMBER . . . your 3-year vision is a work in progress. There are no hard and fast rules. It's meant for you to have fun exploring possibilities . . . and over time turning them into probabilities . . . and then reality.

> **NOTE:** *The WRAR on the following two pages is, as mentioned herein, a crucial tool for developing your business. I encourage you to photocopy, scan or type this out and use it **weekly**.*

Weekly Reflection & Achievements Review   Date: _____

(WRAR)   Name: _____

Keeping a pulse on your week-to-week accomplishments, both big and small, builds momentum on your strengths.

These reports can be extremely beneficial for you, so use them with vigour. Remember, it's *your* version of a fulfilling life . . . so **GET INVOLVED!**

a.   *What do I consider as my 5 top achievements this past week? (work and/or personal)*

1) _____

2) _____

3) _____

4) _____

5) _____

b.   *Why are they significant? (Respond in the same order as above.)*

1) _____

2) _____

3) _____

4) _____

5) _____

c.   *What else could I do in the same areas as above to continue making progress in this direction?*

1) _____

2) _____

3) _____

4) _____

5) _____

d.   *What am I resisting doing?*

1) _____

2) _____

3) _____

e. Which are the 3 most important actions needed this week which, come hell or high-water, I am committed to completing in order to reach my 90-day goals?

1) _____

2) _____

3) _____

f. Doing or having what, specifically, will best move me forward with honouring these commitments?

_____

_____

_____

_____

How do I feel today?

_____

_____

_____

_____

Doing what could help me feel better?

_____

_____

_____

_____

How can Lynne help me move forward faster and more easily this week?

_____

_____

_____

_____

_____

NOTE: Your top 5 achievements of the past week do not need to be of earth-shattering, mountain-moving or cancer-curing magnitude. They simply need to be *your* top 5 achievements.

NOTE: You are definitely resisting doing at least 3 items each and every week, even though it doesn't seem that way. What you identify that you're resisting, also, doesn't have to be of such magnitude that if you stepped into it you'd cure the world of all its ailments. They're simply items that **when** you step into them you will enjoy benefits you don't currently have.

CHAPTER FOUR

Continue Moving Forward . . .
Despite all Roadblocks & Detours

Strategy # 3
FOLLOW THROUGH ON YOUR IDEAS: Understand what **TRULY** stops you

Of all of these *7 Simple Strategies 4 Success* which are key to every successful business, I contend that this 3rd one is *the* most important. Granted, without a vision of your future and your destination and time to map out the route to get there, which you'll get from following the exercises in Strategy #1 and Strategy #2, business owners are lost in the deep waters and just reacting to what comes along day-by-day without a compass or knowing in which direction to point their sails.

Strategy #7 is also of paramount importance because it's the *why bother* of even being in business—that point from which so many small business owners start their businesses yet, failing to have a LIFE outside of the business, they become extremely frustrated and get to the point of wondering why they ever did bother to go out on their own in the first place.

Strategy #3, however, is simply everything. We can envision our ideal lifestyle and we can plan until the cows come home, but only when we follow through on those promises we make to ourselves, our families, our employees and our customers, will we get the results we desire.

I was recently conducting a VIP Intensive coaching session with a gentleman and he said *Lynne, I've made so many promises to my family for so many years now, that I just haven't followed through on, that they no longer believe I'm capable of doing it.*

He's not alone. So many people struggle with this. You've promised to be at a family function, or your children's school functions or sports events. You've promised that if they'll just *hang in there* while you're working all these hard, long hours that you'll make it up to everyone with a wonderful family vacation this year—finally! And then you don't. Besides, why should they "hang in there" all year long for one week of fun? (And that 1-week vacation model for business owners is addressed in Strategy #7.)

Your support team at work has been promised that after this job or that one when you turn the profit that you should get you'll buy that piece of equipment that would make everyone's work a lot easier to do . . . and then you don't.

How does this happen? You always have the best of intentions. You don't want to let anyone down. Worst of all, your being a more plugged-in parent, spouse, family member and your business having that equipment or showing your employees how much you care by throwing some fun parties would benefit you, too. So how is it that year-after-year it seems you just can't afford to follow through on your promises?

The reason, I contend, that this Strategy is the most important of all 7 is because this is the glue that holds your foundation together: Follow-Through. It sounds so simple. Simply do what you say you're going to do. If it were so simple, it wouldn't be such a challenge for all of those struggling small business owners. We say it's because we don't have enough *time*—the one resource that truly is limited, and we have proof that it's true. We spend time every day proving we don't have enough time to do whatever it is we're not doing.

We say it's because we don't have enough *money*—one of those resources that truly is *un*limited. The mints make more money every day. There's money coming in and going out of your business every day. I know that you, too, can think of times when you didn't have enough money for something you really wanted and yet you made it happen. You simply did whatever it took to come up with the money. Yet for these promises you've made, on which you're not following through, you're spending valuable time proving that you simply don't have enough money to follow through on them. Whose "goals" are these promises, anyway? What's the benefit to *you* if/when you do follow through on them?

We even say we can't attend these functions or take that special family or couple vacation because we don't have the proper support to be away from our businesses. Humans are another resource that's *un*limited because these, too, we make every single day. I know you'll argue this one with me: There aren't enough skilled people for you to hire. I've had many a client argue this one with me, as well. The moment you simply **make the decision** to do whatever it is you've promised—to yourself, your family, your employees, whomever—every resource you need simply shows up. In fact, if it's an employee who you haven't found in the last 5 months we've been working together, for example, which you believe is causing you to

- still be exhausted,
- unable to attend your sons' sports events and your family's picnics and
- even causing you to only join your spouse and children at the cottage for 2 long weekends instead of the 2 weeks for which you have the cottage,

yet you simply **make the decision** to attend your sons' games every Tuesday and Thursday evenings and be at the cottage for the entire 2 weeks, you, too, will find yourself telling me:

> *You're never going to believe this, but the day after our coaching session last week a certified*
> *<whatever your trade is> showed up at my door looking for a job.*

This has happened with so many clients that, of course, I believe it. I believed it the first time it happened for a client and I was delighted with the news. Today I just know that it will happen equally quickly for you, too, once you **make the decision**.

You see from before the time you entered this world from your mother's womb, your *operating system* was being programmed. The very people who love you the most, wanting the best for you, did everything in their power, with the tools they had at the time, to keep you safe from all harm. They were constantly telling you to *be careful*, "for your own good". You've learned from all of the examples and stories around you how to behave and how *not* to behave. The sad news is that our parents **loved us to death**, and you're doing it even worse to your children today, because we improve and grow/expand with every generation. You become your mother or your father, you add to what they've taught you everything you've learned through your own experiences and now you're even better at creating your children's *operating system* than your parents in creating yours and their parents were in creating theirs. You'll see this if you just look around and see how many young adults there are today who are, in what I refer to as, *the lost generation*: Mid-twenties, still looking at all their options as to what they want to do and be in life and still unsure. So instead of just getting out there and living life they're still at home with Mom and Dad being *careful* and *safe*.

We could talk more about these young people whose parents have **loved them to death** in Strategy #5—Empower your Support—Lead a Championship Support Team, but for this example I just want to bring to your attention that all of those employee hassles you're having, other small business owners are having with your children, as well. You simply want to give to your children everything you didn't have. I've heard it in all of the workshops I've led over the years. During the breaks I'll overhear a woman and a man, never before having met, discussing this and that always leads me into Strategy #5—the very words my clients in the room are using in discussion with each other.

Your *operating system*, created by your parents, relatives, community leaders, teachers, etc., you've installed in your children with the help of all of their other relatives, community leaders, teachers, etc. In addition to all of your experiences that you've added into your *operating system* your children are doing likewise. This means that when we're looking at our adult children and wondering *Why in heaven's name is (s)he not doing <whatever>?* we need simply remember that it's because we've shown them this by example and taught them that it's more important to stay safe and play small that to run out there and take risks with enough faith in themselves for everything to turn out just as their heart desires.

Let's look at this *operating system* like the operating system in a computer. We turn the computer on in the morning and we really have no idea what it does to make the programs work which we've installed. We just know that the operating system is the foundation of the computer's functioning. And so is it in us. Sadly, however, our operating system never shuts off, the way our computers do when we turn the computer off. For us, when we go to sleep our operating system, which is our subconscious mind, continues to work all night long. Have you ever woken up from a dream and found yourself thinking about it numerous times throughout the day? It was a little disconcerting . . . but it was just a dream. Well, your subconscious mind doesn't know that it was just a dream. Your subconscious mind doesn't know the difference between reality and perception. Perception is reality, until the perceived reality is proven not to be real by replacing it with a different experience.

I don't want to go too deeply into the psychology of the subconscious mind, here, but it does require some mention because it is THE very thing that causes 99% of small businesses to become painful memories for families by year 10. Lack of knowledge and skill can always be compensated for, either by studying or hiring the right people. Money is by no means limited, as I've referred to herein. The "right" people we'll discuss further in Strategy #5.

The Limiting Beliefs in our own personal Belief System is what stops us.

Every organism on this planet is subject to the very same Universal Laws. An amoeba, a tree, a fish, a human, an idea—everything is subject to, among all of the other Universal Laws, the Universal Law of Expansion. Yet, we've been programmed from a very early age—even pre-birth—that we shouldn't expect too much. We should be happy with what we have. People who start developing their minds and broadening their outlook feel that it's somehow their responsibility to concern themselves with saving the less fortunate—whether in their own community or country or countries abroad. By "taking care of others" you're simply avoiding growing yourself. It's none of your concern what those others want for themselves. For you to truly help others, you need to allow them to take care of themselves and allow them to grow—to develop themselves, as they're subject to do through the Universal Law of Expansion—just like yourself. Whenever, in fact, you find yourself focusing on others, it is simply a distraction from focusing on your own growth and development. That's the subconscious mind at work.

You see the function of the subconscious mind is to ensure the person survives. The function of your subconscious mind, therefore, is for your survival. Hence, you are not in any way *responsible* for the survival of another—only for your own. But we've all been taught that it's good to take care of others, worry about others, focus on others' problems and help them solve their problems, give others lots of advice on what to do—which causes us a lot of frustration because they don't want our advice anyway. (I do have two exceptions for this, however: young children and severely mentally or physically challenged adults.)

In that your subconscious mind's function is to ensure you survive, thanks to its programming over all of these decades, every time you decide to do something you haven't already done and succeeded at, your subconscious mind will do everything in its power to stop you. Why? Because *you might die!* If you haven't already done this act (whatever you're about to do for the first time), how do you know you'll survive it? Your subconscious mind doesn't know that you will, so it does everything in its power to stop you . . . and **never underestimate the power of your subconscious mind**. It has the ability to cause you to be sick, to cause you to have accidents and many other things that will stop you, but just look at this. Its fear is that you will die, yet it will cause you to become seriously ill or have an accident to stop you from moving forward . . . but the illness or accident that our subconscious minds "cause us to create" can result in our death.

This is how insidious our subconscious mind is. It makes absolutely NO SENSE. It just has one purpose and it will do everything to fulfil its purpose.

You, on the other hand, also have a purpose and until now . . . if you're struggling to get the results you desire in your business . . . you are NOT doing everything to fulfil your purpose. You, like 97% of the population, are being controlled by your subconscious mind which will make you sick or have you be in an accident to stop you from fulfilling your purpose.

So, as I tell all of my clients when we start into learning this Strategy, it's essential that you know that

You're going to Die!

It happens to all of us eventually. Therefore . . .

It's what you do between THIS VERY MOMENT and that LAST MOMENT that counts.

And this is the very purpose of why I do what I do with and for people like you, such as write this book, train on these strategies, coach people on bringing all of their ideas to fruition. When I was 28 years old, I was making arrangements to leave the father of my children because our marriage had been bad for too many years and it was getting worse. On this day, in particular, I was taking action on my decision to end the marriage (not still thinking about the idea) and that afternoon my older daughter, then 7, and I went cycling. The last thing I remember was seeing our dog suddenly appear, running out of the woods and the next thing I knew I was waking up in a hospital bed in the intensive care unit 2½ days later. Little did I know then what I know now about the power of our subconscious minds, and its insidiousness . . . that it would nearly kill me rather than risk allowing me to have the expansion I wanted . . . because it might die. This is a typical example of the workings of our subconscious mind, but it doesn't always show up in such a clear example. Of course I didn't see this as a clear example of the workings of the subconscious mind back then, either.

For a business owner, the slow and painful death of the business is the workings of the subconscious mind. Whichever excuse(s) you've ever heard someone use for their business not being successful, is merely the workings of the subconscious mind. *Banks won't give you money when you need it and that's why I lost everything.* I've heard this one numerous times. You only got into that situation of needing money that badly because you were shrinking, instead of growing; and why would a bank or anyone lend money to a dying business? It's a bad risk at that point. Remember that Universal Law I mentioned earlier?

The Universal Law of Expansion

Everything on this planet is subject to this and all of the other universal laws. Let's just focus on this one. Trees, animals, plants, fish, amoeba, mold, etc. don't *worry* about growing. They simply do it. They have a system, usually in sync with the seasons and they follow that system all the time—consistently & persistently. Every once in a while a catastrophe comes along, like maybe an ice storm as we had in our area in 1998 where *millions* of trees were split in half. Most didn't stop growing. They just went back down to the foundation of their system and grew stronger and then in a flash, it seemed, within just a few months where all those branches were broken off and their trunks were badly damaged there were chutes and leaves making them look as beautiful as ever. In fewer than 3 years (their 3-year vision, perhaps?) you couldn't even tell that there had been such devastation. We, on the other hand, as humans, have

the *Power of Reasoning* and therein lies our biggest problem.

Because we think, we limit ourselves. If you haven't already started listening to Earl Nightingale's *The Strangest Secret*, which you can find on YouTube, then I recommend you do so. He explains very well how we become what we think about. We believe that we're thinking with our reasoning minds, however we don't, actually. We do think, of course, in our conscious minds—our thinking minds—but we're thinking about what our subconscious minds—our feeling minds—impress upon us to think. By this I mean that we *receive an idea*. We often say: *Hey, I just got an idea*. Where did we get it from, do you imagine? As we start to "think", consciously in our thinking mind, about this idea we start to have a "feeling" about the idea. This "feeling" comes from our "feeling mind"—our subconscious mind. Now, as we continue to think about the idea, the idea takes a very different shape. If our feelings are good, positive, growth-filled then our idea will start to grow. If, on the other hand, our feelings about the idea are negative, limiting, squashing, then our idea will start to shrink and may even die right there on the vine.

Here's the thing about using our feelings to think about ideas—any types of ideas, but especially ideas for growing our businesses.

Our FEELINGS are simply memories.

We cannot have a feeling about anything unless we've already experienced it, right? If we haven't already experienced something then we can't have a feeling about it, because we don't know about it first-hand. Are you following me? And because we actually have a feeling about **everything**, this means that we're putting a feeling on this new idea, this new opportunity, that doesn't even belong, because it's a new experience to us. We've never "been there/done that" before so since we've neither succeeded nor failed with this before . . . we can't possibility have a feeling about it. It should be neutral, with no feeling whatsoever.

Because we apply a feeling to this new thought, idea, opportunity, we're painting this new opportunity—something we've never experienced before—with the memory of something else. How foolish is this? And we do it all the time. An example is trying a new food. How many times have you had to convince young children that they just might like it if only they'd try this new food with an open mind? We do the same thing . . . *with business ideas!* Worse yet, with our *very own* great business ideas.

So, given that our feelings are nothing but memories and that we apply our feelings to ideas as we *think about* them, we're actually, now, *making decisions* for the future of our business *from the past*. How logical is that?

Our subconscious mind is 90% of our mind and remember: Our subconscious mind is our "feeling" mind. Of most importance as you change the way you consider ideas and make decisions, it's essential that you remember that feelings are merely memories. In fact, we only remember things about which we had a feeling (an emotion). If our emotions were not stirred up in the incident then the incident wouldn't get lodged in our memory bank. This is not only for negative emotions, but positive as well. So memories only get saved in our operating system because we had a strong feeling about it and all of our feelings . . . which comprise 90% of our mind . . . are only memories.

While we think our conscious mind may be the remaining 10% of our mind, let's leave some space for our super-conscious mind—that higher part of us through which our ideas come. At the moment, if you don't follow your intuition too much, then your super-conscious mind may only be developed in the 1-2% range. Trust me on this one: This part of you can easily be developed to be much higher and I encourage you to develop it. This makes **decision-making** so much easier, so much faster and a heck of a lot more fun!

Recognizing Intuition

Because I'm frequently asked about recognizing intuition, I'll give you an example. One client was given the exercise of paying attention to positive thoughts that came to her that week (as opposed to negative, limiting, "be careful" types of thoughts). This is what she reported in with:

As I was running all of my errands on Thursday, as usual, I saw this sandwich-board in front of a carwash and this thought came to me: I should get my car washed here. I always get my car washed at Harry's place, though, and I like to be loyal to other small businesses, just as I like them to be loyal to me, so I ignored the idea and carried on. At the end of my errands, as usual, I go to Harry's carwash and you're never going to believe it! Harry's carwash was out-of-order! I then had to drive all the way back across town to get my car washed. Is that what you mean by intuition, Lynne? "Bingo!"

And this is what I encourage you, as well, to enhance in yourself. Take action on these ideas, small like this one or much bigger . . . I mean MUCH bigger, like buying that 2nd business . . . and you'll see yourself being far more productive in all aspects of your business and in your personal life. Look at the time this woman would have saved with that one idea alone, had she only said YES to it. I totally agree with the old adage that time is money. When you start making decisions much faster you'll being saving a lot of time . . . and money.

Your exercise for Strategy #3 is to improve your Decision-Making system. One business owner, with whom I've had the privilege of being a partner in growing his business for numerous years now, still makes some decisions somewhat slowly, but now it's only for the first time he's ever done something that the decision is made "somewhat" slowly (albeit a lot faster than just a few short years ago!). And that said, decisions are now being made and being acted upon, and that, in itself, is a huge improvement for this small business owner. I find that most small businesses struggle because

> *the vast majority of Small Business Owners make decisions very slowly . . .*
> *and then drag their heels when taking action on the decision.*

Why? Because

1. They lack self-confidence;
2. They lack **proper** support; and,
3. They lack accountability.

Most of us went into business for ourselves because we're great at our trade. That's why I went into business. How about you? As a professional coach, and now as a trainer of these business strategies . . . and especially training on what stops us from thinking BIG and daring to do *whatever the heck it takes* to receive our HEART'S DESIRES . . . I had TONS of self-confidence. Initially, I didn't have a lot of confidence when it came to being an entrepreneur, so I did *whatever the heck it took* to gain that confidence; and each time I feel myself slowing down and not moving forward as quickly as I want to, I get the support I need to get moving again at the speed I desire.

Many of the people reading this book, in fact, may be considering hiring a business & mindset coach to work with in person, yet they will drag their heels on it for a long time to come before ever actually taking that step, if they ever do.

Why? Because

1. Many of the readers of this book lack the confidence to make the decision . . . because their subconscious minds just heard them consciously thinking about it and quickly splashed a thick coat of memory on the idea, and there they stop. It may have been the memory of a gossiping party about someone in their neighbourhood who spent money on something that your parents and all of your Aunts and Uncles thought was a foolish idea. There was such a hen's party about it, that it left an impression on your subconscious mind . . . and this perception became your reality.

2. Many of the readers of this book lack proper support or else they would take this idea to their spouse or business partner or mentor or bank manager and tell these people on their "championship support team" they have *decided* to work personally with a business coach. If that person on your support team truly is supportive (s)he will encourage you on your decision. While redoing his contract, in common language that he could explain more easily to his customers, one of my clients mentioned to his lawyer that he was now working with a business coach. His lawyer tried to talk him out of working with me, saying: *I can help you with anything you need help with in your business! You don't need a business coach!* A lawyer, of all people! This lawyer, like many, is someone whose office is filled with papers piled everywhere, leaving my clients wondering if that's why he's often late for his appointments, because he can't find their documents. This lawyer is someone who seldom returns phone calls promptly and seems to get things done at the last moment. And this *is* someone who's on their "championship support" team. As a lawyer he is. As a business strategies trainer and a business improvement and growth advisor, an accountability partner to help these fine folks follow through on their ideas, he definitely isn't. Our mutual clients' business had been struggling for a decade and now, in less than 2 years they're seeing profits that make them feel giddy at times; profits that had eluded them over their first decade in business, with the *help* of

this supportive lawyer and others who weren't the **proper support** of which I'm speaking here.

3. Many of the readers of this book lack accountability so even with this support if you don't follow through—so what? Imagine this lawyer being supportive and holding these clients accountable to following through on their business growth ideas when their subconscious minds have them gripped in fear—and these folks have been gripped in fear numerous times over the last 22 months as they've taken their business from between repeated financial losses/no profit/minimal profit in the last 10 years to well over $100K in profit in the 2nd year of working with a business & mindset coach.

This is just one example of saying YES to an idea and taking immediate action on it, but it's a perfect one. How many ideas flit through your mind in the course of a day? How many do you consider . . . and then never really make a decision on one way or the other? How many do you just instantly LOVE and say "YES" to . . . or instantly dislike and say "NO" to? How many do you take **immediate** action on?

If you have to think twice about something . . . don't bother.

Over the next month keep track of

*   The number of ideas that do flit through your mind. Carry a pocket-sized or purse-sized notebook around with you at all times, which I call an ***Ideas Book*** (see how simple everything is in these teachings?). Each time an idea passes through your mind write it down. Remember: Ideas are like slippery fish. If you don't gaff them with the end of your pen they'll get away on you (as one of my mentor's mentor says).

*   Schedule 15 minutes each week to review your ***Ideas Book*** and identify the number of those ideas that flitted through your mind that you actually considered.

*   Likewise, identify the number of those ideas on which you took action . . . all the way to fruition.

IDEA . CONSIDER . DECIDE . ACT

How quickly do you go from start to finish in this process? Here's an example:

Case Study

A client had an idea of purchasing a business that complemented his existing, now flourishing, business. He had no actual business in mind to buy. He had just received the idea to grow his business by purchasing a complementary one.

As we discussed his idea, I asked him: Is this something you want?

> "Yes,"

(followed by lots and lots of reasoning why—only for the sake of his subconscious mind, not for my sake. I encourage you to simply ask yourself: Is this something I want? And the answer is to be a simple "Yes" or "No".)

The Decision, therefore, was "Yes". It could just have easily been "No", but in this case, it wasn't (obviously, or I wouldn't have chosen this as the example, right?).

A Decision is only an IDEA . . .

unless followed by IMMEDIATE action.

Without action, you really haven't made a decision. You've simply considered the idea. In a case without action, you have a situation where the idea is still swirling around in your mind, because YES, it's something you want. And then, such as in John's case, after 6 years his brother-in-law threatens to punch him in the face if he ever mentions that idea again because he's sick to death of hearing about it. It was at that point that John connected with me and within 6 months we had his business idea all mapped out and being acted upon.

Now, on the other hand, in the example above where my client "decided" to purchase an existing business to complement his own, the immediate action/first step required was simply to put out feelers (discreetly to his accountant and lawyer, for example). Inside of a year from the time of this coaching session where my client was pursuing his "idea" and after making a decision to go forward he then put out some "feelers", a perfect business was presented to my client. Thanks to having proper support in the form of an accountant and a lawyer who knew what he was looking for, and a business coach to help keep him moving, he took immediate action and became the proud owner of this sizeable business within 2 months.

Not all decisions bear fruit instantaneously, but if you currently desire business results you don't currently have then I can guarantee you that improving your decision-making system will see you receiving much better business results *immediately*.

Which type of decision-maker would you say you are?

1. One who makes decisions very slowly (you're stuck in your subconscious mind's FEAR) or
2. One who, after saying "YES" to your idea, either
   a. does not have the proper support or
   b. does not have a strong accountability partner.

Most small business owners have neither, I can assure you of this. You often look to your spouse to be your cheerleader and support person, and for various reasons this is not a role your spouse is suited for or it's not a role your spouse even wants. Have you asked him/her? Oftentimes when one of my clients bounces an idea off his/her spouse, the response is one of fear, lack, limitation—not from my client's subconscious mind, but from the spouse's. *How can you possibly think of offering that kind of salary to someone else? You don't even make that much every year?* Had this business owner *not* been engaged in a "proper support" partnership with a business coach, do you think he would have hired that key person in his business? Within 6 months that person had paid for himself, but my client's wife couldn't see that as a sure thing. And had we not continued to work together until after that 6-month period, ensuring the follow-through of all of the changes necessary in the business to make this acquisition profitable, the hiring of that key person may well have had very different results—the type of results this spouse was accustomed to seeing from her husband's "big" business ideas, which was the cause for her concern.

To ensure you *follow through* on every one of your lucrative ideas it's essential that you *hold yourself visibly accountable* . . . typically to someone other than just your spouse or even your employees.

I recommend that every business owner have a business coach, and one who's strong on mindset. I know you think you can't afford a business coach. From the business improvements and growth I've seen with every one of the several hundreds of clients I've coached, I can guarantee you that you *cannot afford **not** to have a business success coach.* Why would we choose to continue to struggle, when we can get there (wherever "there" is for you, as in Strategy #1) *faster* & and a heck of a lot more ***easily*** than by working at it alone?

I also recommend that every business owner have a mentor. Your business coach doesn't need to come from your industry—and I contend that the best coach for you does *not* come from your industry—but your mentor should be someone who does; someone who's *been there & done that.* It's quite simple to find a mentor. Who do you look up to in your area and in your industry? Why not invite this person to lunch? Ask for their advice. *Everyone loves to be asked to give advice!* Ask if they'd be agreeable to go to lunch with you every now and again—monthly or quarterly. You'll be pleasantly surprised, I'm sure, to learn how agreeable this person will be to your invitation and to answer your questions about how they dealt with the sorts of challenges you're currently struggling with.

Cheerleaders are an essential part of every successful business. There are enough people out there who see the cup half empty. You want to surround yourself with people who see the cup half full and who are working on filling their own cup. It's enough of a challenge on a day-to-day basis, while improving your business results, to stay focused on only the positive aspects of a negative Profit & Loss Statement; to stay focused on your cash-flow improving when at this precise moment it's really bad. We owe it to ourselves NOT to be surrounded by people who only see the challenges in life, helping to drag you down with them.

Here are some very simple (though not necessarily easy) steps to take starting *right now:*

1. Simply stop spending your valuable time with anyone outside of work and family who isn't upbeat and positive. (This doesn't mean you can't console a friend who's dealing with a tragedy, but it does mean to stop listening to those friends who gossip and complain and with whom you agree and commiserate!)
2. Explain to your family what you're focusing on accomplishing with your business, from following the exercises in this book, and how it will benefit them. Then explain that there's a new policy around home from now on related to increasing the cheerleading and support for you and the business that not only feeds them but will give them all these benefits you mentioned. This new policy could be as simple as everyone needing to share a win that they had that day—and everyone else must be supportive of that person and cheerful about their win. You know the type of improvement that would best serve your family, but if you have any doubts (that good old subconscious mind again), simply listen to your intuition.

3. Likewise, explain to everyone in your business what you're focusing on and tell each of them, specifically, individually or as a group, how they can best support you. There is a lot of negative chit-chat in businesses these days and yours may be the same. As in the example for your family you may want to suggest that everyone in your business share a win with everyone else. When they start looking for WINs, they'll find many more of them.

4. We'll add customers to this list when we get to Strategy #6, but in the meantime, only hire on new customers for their ability to help you grow *your* business—not just for the money you think you'll make to alleviate your cash-flow problem. The headaches are far more costly than the interest on your line-of-credit.

So, to summarize Strategy #3—If you were to FOLLOW THROUGH 100% on every single BUSINESS GROWTH idea you had from here on in, you would never struggle again in your business. I'm not saying challenges wouldn't arise. I'm not saying you will always feel "comfortable" when stepping out of your comfort zone and into these opportunities. I'm saying that with **proper support**, with a strong accountability partner who won't allow you to accept less than you deserve from yourself anymore, and with your renewed self-confidence, knowing your subconscious mind limits your belief in yourself, you would have the FAITH in yourself to do *whatever the heck it takes* to . . .

Receive EVERYTHING your Heart Desires.

CHAPTER FIVE

Leave Your Financial Fears Behind

Strategy # 4
TAME THE CASH-FLOW BEAST: Get over your FEAR of Debt

Are you playing to win in your business? Or, like 80% of small business owners,

are you playing not to lose?

I've already mentioned the staggering statistics of how few small businesses are still in business at the 4-year mark: only 10%; and how by year 10 only 1% of our businesses are still in operation . . . yet for those of us who are still around at the 10-year mark a staggering 80% of those 1% are still struggling.

Bank Managers will tell you the reason is due to your not managing your finances properly.

I agree with Bankers, in that small business owners do lack financial control. I have delivered presentations, led seminars and facilitated ½-day and full-day workshops to people like you since early 2005. Every single time I ask

"Who, here, has a family budget?"

Maybe surprisingly to you, there are always fewer than 10% of the people in the room who raise their hands. How about you? Do you and your life partner have a family budget . . . which you follow?

"Who here operates their business from annual projections—a business budget?"

Even fewer than those 10% in these seminars and workshops who have a family budget raise their hands and there may be just one person in the room who has both.

I've only twice had defensive reasoning offered up, and both times by women, to explain, on behalf of the group, why so few work from a budget.

> *"Because we don't want to have our spending limited.*
> *We already work so hard, the least we should be able to do is buy whatever we want."*

"And do you buy *everything* you want?" I've asked in both cases. "Well, no. I can't do that!"

If you invest yourself in this chapter, you will come to understand how simple it can be for you to actually be able to buy yourself, and those on whom you want to shower gifts, ***everything you want to buy.***

FREEDOM is NEVER looking at a PRICE-TAG again!

Now that statement comes with this **warning**:

> ***If you invest yourself*** *in this chapter—and in every chapter of this book—with your new understanding of*
> - o *what stops you and*
> - o *the way to simply step past those blockages;*
> - o *what causes you and your family to struggle and*
> - o *how to bring your struggles to an end,*
>
> *then your business will* ***provide the lifestyle*** *you've only dreamt of before—or maybe haven't even allowed yourself to dream of as in my case and the case of many of my clients—allowing you and your family to have everything your heart desires with all the time you want in which to enjoy it.*

Now please permit me to explain why I say that the earlier statement comes with a warning:

Case Study

> A couple who'd owned and operated their own business, from start-up in their home for some 18 years, whose children were now teenagers whom they enjoyed taking all over the place for their sports games, came to me for help in

growing their business without all the challenges. They, like a good number of my clients, knew it was time to take the business out of the house and they were afraid to do it. They had become such a well-respected company that the status quo was simply too much and changes needed to be made.

In our very first VIP Intensive coaching session, which was the start of us being in partnership for nearly a year-and-a-half, we looked at everything, as we always do. I recall their wanting to improve their spending habits, especially the wife's, and I gave them suggestions/possibilities on making improvements. I was explaining to them at that time that

We can have everything our hearts desire.

However, rather than the system they used (the system maybe 95% of the population uses): Put it on plastic and worry about paying it later; I recommended they simply make the purchase, even on plastic, and then

Do *whatever the heck it takes* to bring that money in.

I even recommended, as I have to many small business owners, that she put all of her plastic cards into a metal can of water and put them into the freezer. Then, should she decide on a whim to buy something that, as she said, *she didn't even really want or like*, she would have to wait until the water thawed by placing the can on the counter to be able to retrieve her credit cards to make use of them. This would, literally, provide her with a cooling down period and she may refrain from making purchases which she, herself, calls foolish and useless.

A good 12 months later that couple and I were in conversation again specifically about their debt-load and they were admitting to me that while their business results had dramatically improved, their debt-load was higher today than it had ever been before—even 12 months earlier when it was the topic of discussion brought up by them. Ok, that may be reasonable given the investments they had made over the year by taking their business out of the house. When we got to the bottom of it, I was being told: "*Lynne, remember when you told me I needed to make it difficult for me to buy those useless items? Well, when you said I could have anything my heart desires, that's all I could hear all year and I bought even more junk than I normally did. I've spent 10s of 1,000s of dollars on utter junk! And I owe for it all! We've had a really FUN year, and we needed that fun after all these years in business, but this is crazy what I've gotten us into,"* she said, *"and the worst of it is that the phone's not even ringing!"*

We then looked at this age-old problem small business owners have when they grow their businesses. When the business was in their home the phone rang what felt like frequently because it was in their home, and it had become overwhelming to them. Now that they're in a big space downtown they *want* that phone to ring so frequently that their secretary is busy full-time answering it.

As we were looking at the various extremely simple marketing tactics which I'll share with you in Strategy #6, in answer to my questions about "what had been done in relation to this?" and "what had been done in relation to that?", I consistently & persistently heard: *That doesn't work for me.* By about the 4th such response I asked: *How does bankruptcy work for you?*

As my clients will tell you: I'm forthright; I'm strict; I'm tell-it-like-it-is; I'm kind; I'm compassionate; I'm gentle; I'm tough. Essentially, I am however you need me to be to help you get **the heck out of your own way** so that you can enjoy the results that ***your heart desires***. The results these clients were currently faced with were not what their hearts desired, but they were the results they were settling for. And I was helping them see what the results would look like when they grew if they were to continue travelling down that same path, because as I've explained already

Everything on this planet is subject to the Universal Law of Expansion . . .
even debt.

So when I say that this book is the tool that can help you live the lifestyle you've only ever dreamt of before, I'm serious. This tool, however, must be used in its entirety . . . not just the pages or phrases you like. You see, it's those very actions we **RESIST** doing that are the actions that will give us the success we're after. What we **RESIST** persists, because it is the very obstacle that's blocking our path to success. Overcome these obstacles which you're currently resisting . . . that you've been resisting (afraid of) for years . . . and every new obstacle that comes along will be as simple as soft butter to cut through.

You are never sent a **DESIRE** without **THE WAY to realize the desire** also being shown to you once you say "Yes" to the desire/opportunity/idea. Our challenge is "seeing" *the way* and saying "Yes" to it.

I understand this and that's why I'm so compassionate as my clients come to understand it for yourself. As I know oh, so well, we quickly answer the question I taught you in the previous chapter under Strategy #3, about the DESIRE:

Is this something I want? with a YES . . . and then you'll explain "how" this desire is to come to you. I know this because a couple of years ago after a short time I became consciously aware that I was doing this yet again—even though by now I *knew* better and I understood the consequences. That means that you've said a "conditional" YES in answer to the question. You didn't answer YES—you answered: YES, but MY way.

And just like the woman I spoke of above, I, too, struggled with the opportunity/idea/desire with which I was presented because I said "YES . . . in 6 months' time (in MY time)." During those 6 months I had a huge obstacle come my way that could not possibly have come along had I said YES, simply YES and stepped into the opportunity right then.

So to use the tools I'm offering you through this book, use ALL of the facets of the tool— PRECISELY as directed.

Getting back to the budgets, my logic for using budgets and recommending that you develop the same habit is because a budget . . . which includes absolutely everything like

- luxury vacations,
- special events like taking your oldest child turning 16 away for a few days, which you want to make a family tradition for the younger children, as well,
- gifts,
- toys / rewards,
- long weekends for the couple,
- everything your hearts desire . . . will tell you what your annual income needs to be to make that budget a reality, as opposed to a wish-list (or a restriction as the 2 women mentioned in workshops).

Creating a Simple Family Household Budget

The template: A family budget doesn't have to be complicated. Either find one on the internet, write to **info@mljcoaching.com** and request one from us or simply make a list of all of your family's expenditures.

1. Track all of your expenses, for the entire family, for 3 months. Keep receipts for everything. Pretend you're the government auditing your family's books! Be that diligent. It's for the benefit of your entire family, after all.

2. At the end of the 3 months create categories into which all of the expenditures you and your entire family incurred can be lumped. Do it on a simple Excel Spreadsheet, if that's easy for you.

3. The key . . . is to follow the budget. You're the one who created it, so there are no surprises. It's time to get strict with yourself . . . for the benefit of your entire family's wellbeing.

4. Now, that amount that you see as the total figure for the year on that family budget is, at a minimum, the income you are now targeting to receive this year—**after tax**. To do that you need to know what your projected annual sales figure needs to be, which will cover all of your projected expenditures in the business, including your new salary and your income tax.

PLAN FOR A RAINY DAY and you'll get a rainy day

Do you currently have a sum equal to 3 months' expenditures available to you, without any stress? I don't believe in *planning for a rainy day* because

WHAT WE FOCUS ON WE CREATE

and therefore I do not suggest that you focus on preparing yourself for having a rainy day. I do not want you to fixate on accumulating savings that are just going to sit there in a bank account, never being used for anything more than to make you feel comfortable . . . keeping you well inside your comfort zone.

However, it goes without saying that your customers could be those types of folks who listen to the news every time there's some fear-mongering going on about *the worst global economy we've seen in years and it's likely to be with us for more than a decade!* (such as I just recently heard on the Australian Broadcasting Corporation's radio network while driving into Cairns.) If your customers do listen to that sort of stuff, they're going to require a lot more of your time and attention to help them stay focused on growing their businesses by hiring your services, and this could cause a slow-down in your operation.

Should this ever happen to you (because I know that since you've purchased this book you wouldn't dare be the type of small business owner who watches that fear-mongering on television anymore or listens to it on the radio, reads it in papers or especially allows people to discuss it around you!) . . . but should you find your customers buying into that belief system, you will want to be able to continue growing your business with minimal stress by having a **RESERVE** of cash-on-hand. By so doing, this will give you time to regroup, listen to the new ideas that come to you, re-strategize and invest more of your energy in working with better quality customers—such as the type who look at fear-mongering and media glooming-and-dooming as an opportunity. Do you realize that this gloom-and-doom news is enhanced by the media and splashed on front pages because it sells ads, due to the mass population loving bad news? Your having a 3-month financial buffer is just another one of the essential components for acquiring financial control in your business. Let's explore some more of the Essential Steps in Strategy #4 on which I train and coach my clients:

4 ESSENTIAL STEPS FOR ACQUIRING and/or MAINTAINING FINANCIAL CONTROL

1. **Create Budgets**
2. **Create Monthly Management Accounts**
3. **Get Your Prices Right**
4. **Reduce Debt while you Create Reserves**

1. Create Budgets [on a personal and professional basis]—as discussed above

2. Create Monthly Management Accounts—Depending on the size of your business you may be the one who does all of the bookkeeping and (heaven forbid) your annual taxes—or you may have a full-time comptroller. Either way, owners of small businesses, and the bigger they are the more challenged they are, are the guiltiest parties of NOT reviewing their monthly profit & loss statements.

Let me step back just a moment here in case you're like many of the first few 100 clients I worked with, and still some today, who do their own bookkeeping.

Why are you doing this? I'd like to help you unveil the truth here. Get serious. Why? Truly—why are you your own bookkeeper? If you tell me it's because you love bookkeeping, then I want to hear that sentence finished off with *". . . and because I am a bookkeeper for hire."* Get it? I have worked with plumbers, electricians, masons, builders, renovators, graphic artists, photographers, boat builders, etc. who do their own books. Some actually tell me it's because they enjoy working with numbers. "Then get your accounting degree and make real money at it!" I say, "because you're paying a bookkeeper who's not even good at it $65/hour (an electrician's billable rate)." Yes, at the end of the conversation this electrician realized it's because he was afraid to have to pay someone $25/hour to do his books . . . and he was doing them late at night, missing many of the small items used on the jobs and sometimes forgetting to bill clients all together!

If you own a business that's not a bookkeeping business, and you're doing your bookkeeping I encourage you to open your agenda *right now* and mark an appointment in it for tomorrow morning to call someone you know who knows of a freelance bookkeeper you can hire. Go ahead . . . **Do it NOW!** It's essential that we ALL stick to our brilliance and let others enjoy making a living by utilizing theirs.

STICK TO WHAT YOU DO BEST and Hire Out the REST.

This goes for housecleaning, laundry, cleaning your office, your trucks, running errands, getting your truck serviced—everything. Look at what your hourly rate truly is, as an entrepreneur, not a technician, and know that you are paying $150/hour (your entrepreneurial hourly rate, at a minimum) for a service delivery person, a bookkeeper, a housekeeper, etc.

So, now that you're not doing your books anymore, you do want to have a monthly meeting with yourself to review them. This was well covered in the Chapter on Strategy #2.

Look at your Financial Results and be sure to make any course corrections necessary. For example you may find you've allowed in your Annual Projections for some maintenance on vehicles, but one is using more than its share. Is it time, maybe, to purchase a new vehicle, or make an extensive repair? If so, it's time to edit your annual projections.

3. **Get your Prices Right**: When was the last time you increased your rates? I recommend to you right now exactly what I recommend to each and every one of my clients when we first meet:

Increase your prices tomorrow morning by 10%.

And do this even if you're about to tell me: *But I just increased my prices a few weeks ago.* Do it again now! And increase your rates again by another 10% or better 3 months from now. I've been encouraging my clients to increase their rates by 10% for many years, now, and with every single client they tell me within a couple of months that not one single client bat an eyelid (made a complaint). This is why I say to continue to increase your rates *until you do* cause someone to ask questions.

A young couple who'd been in a 1-on-1 private coaching partnership with me for a couple or 3 months already asked me what they should be charging as the bill-out rate. *"I don't know,"* I responded. *"What are other businesses like yours in your area charging?"*

They didn't know. Hmmmm . . . that response in itself was cause for alarm. Yes, they were a very young couple and had only been in business for about 5 years at the time but you may be surprised how many people who've been in businesses for more than a decade—and 2 decades, even—who can't tell me what *they should be charging.* How about you? What is the going rate for your business' services? How close to that rate are you billing right now? And be careful of only charging "the norm". That indicates to purchasers that your service/products are also "the norm." The type of customers you want in your business want *better than the norm*, and in order for you to communicate to them that you provide higher quality services/products, your pricing must reflect that.

I encouraged these young entrepreneurs do so some research that week to find out how their bill-out rate compared to others in their sector of the industry and in their catchment area. They were practically levitating when we connected the following week for our coaching session! What were they so excited about? *"It's not as exciting as it is scary!"* the young man said.

They had done some research, in various forms, and it all proved to them that their billable rate was 50% what all other businesses in their sector and geographical area were charging! How did their rates get to be that out-of-whack? Well, when they started the business he knew he was charging less but he was just new in business and felt it was reasonable. During the following 5 years he'd never checked again. Now he was charging 50% and delivering at least as good as the "top dogs" and providing much better services than at least half of the local businesses.

"What do I do now? I can't just double my rates!!!"

"You can't? What's stopping you?" They both reflected and decided they could, but not immediately. "Where will you start?" was my question. Again, this is an example of how a good professional business coach does *NOT* tell a client what to do. Why not? Because had I told this young couple to go out and double their rates that week, they would have done it with such fear and lack of confidence that their clients would have sensed that something wasn't right . . . and they likely would have ended up losing a lot of good customers, and confirmed that, as their doubts/fears/subconscious mind had them believing: it would be impossible to succeed in business if they were to raise their rates so dramatically.

Therefore, by the owners of the business making the decision as to the amount by which they'd increase their rates . . . which they did, at a 50% increase to start . . . they informed their customers with confidence, feeling very justified in charging the increased amount. The result was that only one customer had a problem with it (and after a few months he approached them again). And immediately, every new customer that signed a contract with them was charged a 100% increase than had they signed the contract just a few weeks earlier. Within no more than 6 months they had all of their customers up to the 100% increase in rates and today they're still doing annual research to be sure their rates are in line with providing the best services in their area, guaranteeing that their customers have a pleasant experience dealing with them.

By how much should you be increasing your rates? _____

On which date are you increasing your rates? _____

In the event I haven't succeeded in impressing upon you the simplicity of increasing your rates, here's yet another example of how simple it was. When a mechanical service contractor, who served many restaurants and convenience stores through annual contracts, entered into a coaching partnership with me, as always, I asked right off the hop:

"What needs to be done to ensure you receive at least a triple ROI in your partnership with me?"

I know that the increased quality of life, alone, is worth far more than the investment my clients make in themselves through business coaching, but I always like to see *measurable* results—and how better to measure increase than with numbers, right?

So this service provider felt that if he increased his rates across the board that that alone would give him triple the ROI of his financial investment in coaching for 6 months (initial program)— because while he would be increasing his rates this year, he would also create a system for annual increases. *"When was the last time you increased your rates in your Service Agreements?"* He couldn't even tell me, until the following week, when he humbly said that for some customers it had been 4 years and for others up to 10 years. ***"What?!?"*** I try very diligently not to show shock or surprise with my clients, because you could perceive it to be that I am passing negative judgement on you and you may feel inferior or stupid. But honestly, as I explained this to this client—*How could you NEVER have increased your annual rates?* His reasoning: *"I've just been too busy and, as you say, Lynne, 'it never became a priority'."*

We made it a priority. Some of those customers actually had a problem of having their first-ever rate increase, so it was easy to drop them as customers, right? Unfortunately, all of those folks wanted to come back within the next few weeks, but with proper support my client was able to stick to his guns and not take those "D" customers back into his business. (Explained in Strategy 6)

I don't even recall how many hundreds of contracts this amounted to, nor the annual profit generated by these contracts, nor the increase, specifically, but suffice to say that that one change alone covered their entire investment of working with me over the first year-and-a-half, it easily made the monthly instalments on his new "dream truck" and it paid for one of those "adult" toys I mentioned earlier herein, that they have been enjoying using every summer since. Just that contract rate increase alone also paid for at least 3 couple-vacations during that time—vacations they weren't even taking before this.

I do hope that I've made a solid case for how simple it is to increase our rates—as well as the *why bother to do it.* I won't even use my own business as an example, but suffice to say that I no longer have any qualms on raising my rates, especially thanks to the results my clients receive as a result of working with me.

4. **Reduce Debt while you Create Reserves**—I explained earlier the importance of creating a 3-month reserve, so that as your market changes or any business or family incident arises or opportunities appear you can simply step into whatever happens without changing stride. Having this buffer, as I explained, allows you to continue without lots of stress and worry.

While creating our reserves, of course, it's essential, as well, to reduce our debt. The debt I mentioned earlier where the woman has admitted that a lot of valueless purchases she's made are now being carried in the form of debt are the types of debt I encourage you to pay off completely . . . immediately. As you can imagine, this is what I call **Stupid Debt**. I'm sure you have debt that I would call **Smart Debt**—debt that allows you to grow your business by using the bank's money for purchases such as a vehicle, or other equipment, investing in yourself by working with a business coach, that helps you make more money to repay the debt.

I encourage you to repay all Debt, starting with eliminating the **Stupid Debt** first. By doing so you will feel accomplished, by having fewer payments to make each month, and by reducing your carrying (interest) charges, as well as a sense of accomplishment for no longer paying interest charges on frivolous purchases.

On which day will you be studying your financial picture and creating a system for Reducing your Debt while Creating a 3-month Reserve? Date: _____

The benefits of incorporating these new habits I've mentioned herein, at a minimum, are:

- ✓ increased sense of control
- ✓ increased self-esteem and self-confidence
- ✓ significant drop in stress levels
- ✓ the ability to say "no" to taking on jobs you might otherwise have done *just for the money.*

What got us into this position in the first place?

You've been taught to be afraid of money . . . **because that's in our upbringing.** At least 97% of the population operates from this type of family education / upbringing. I know you have, whether you see it yet or not, because every single one of my clients becomes free when they see the connection for themselves. When I learned this, I could easily accept that there was a good possibility that I was afraid of money, but when I realized what the story was around it I was completely taken aback!

The long and short of it is that we are all taught, if not directly by our parents, then just through the media, even, that *money is sinful.*

- Money can't buy happiness.
- Unnecessary decadent items that give us pleasure, such as chocolate, are **sinfully rich**.
- The rich keep getting richer and the poor keep getting poorer (which category do you feel a part of when you hear that expression?).
- Rich people get rich off the backs of others.
- Rich people get rich off the backs of the poor.

Are you now starting to see why it is that most small business owners struggle?

People struggle to stay small. Isn't that peculiar? We're not struggling to grow our businesses. We're struggling to ***stop our businesses from growing.*** We're struggling to stay in that category of people that our community will like, those "hard workers" that everyone praises. You intrinsically know that when you ***grow,*** and start tapping some of your currently untapped potential, others . . . those people with whom you surround yourself . . . will have a problem with it. Not all of your friends and family will, but certainly many of them will—and you even know which ones they are. Don't you? A few of them just came to mind.

Sadly, we struggle to ***not*** live up to our potential, because our potential would amaze us, amaze all those around us, cause us to be much wealthier than we are today and then . . . we would find ourselves in that category about whom your mother and aunts and father and uncles talked about, discussing how "they used to be nice people until they got rich and now just look at them." Your mother and aunts, father and uncles and your grandparents and everyone else who loves you the most, whom you admire, have struggled their whole lives, as well, because that gave them the pride of being "hard workers".

Whenever I'm talking to a prospective client, a small business owner, I ask them what their struggles are. NEVER have I heard someone say: *Lynne, my biggest struggle is to stay at the income and wealth level I'm currently at.* Yet, that is precisely what they are struggling with . . . and **that's all we struggle with**. This has been a huge eye-opener for me as I've come to understand this while crossing that bridge of awareness, through different experiences. I have become very painfully aware of the fact that every struggle I've endured in my lifetime was created by me ***in order to keep me in my place.*** Not the place I truly desired to be. No, the place I had decided . . . as a young child . . . through my conditioning, was the "safest" for me.

> ***What if you could become wealthy and still be a good person . . .***
> ***in the eyes of those you love and who love you most . . . and, most importantly, in your own eyes?***
>
> ***Would you then do whatever the heck it takes to get out of your own way . . .***
> ***and stop struggling?***

CHAPTER SIX

Invite Only Supportive People to Your New Destination

Strategy # 5
HIRE, TRAIN, DEVELOP THEM . . . THEN DELEGATE: Lead a Championship Support Team

One of the biggest problems a self-employed person has is handing over the reins to his staff. Why is this? Because your staff isn't competent . . . or because they're not trustworthy? Either way, why are they still there?

Case Study

> When a group of electrical contractors heard me ask that question at a presentation I was delivering to their Contractor Committee one person listened very carefully to those questions above. Our paths crossed a couple of months later and he said "I know you don't know who I am but something you said a couple of months ago changed my life."
>
> Wow! What the heck could that have been, I asked. He explained that he'd been tolerating an employee who he believed cheated on his time card, yet he felt he couldn't confront him on it because

1. He didn't have solid proof; and, more importantly,
2. He didn't have anyone with whom to replace this person if the person quit right then and there.

He'd been tolerating this employee's questionable trustworthiness for nearly 2 years now! After hearing how blunt I was in my presentation, asking him why he wasn't handing the reins over to this employee, he felt he had permission, in some way, to now deal with this problem. And so he did.

That very next week he gathered the proof he felt he needed for the meeting with this employee, he had the meeting one morning and the employee didn't choose to leave right then: The employer demanded he leave right then. Within a week this untrustworthy electrician had been replaced by someone who was still working in that business the last time we spoke—some 4 years later!

Case Study

When working on staffing issues with one of my clients he told me that his employees

- ended their days whenever they felt like it;
- came to work only if they felt like it, which made scheduling a nightmare;
- and abused the use of cell phones and gas cards.

Why did he tolerate this behaviour? Due to the shortage of skilled tradespeople, my client felt, just like this person to whom I referred above, that his staff had the upper hand. What would he do if one or some quit?

My client took back control by creating a written staffing policy, which was signed by everyone. Sure it was tested, but thanks to the outside professional support he had while creating the staffing policy, he was very clear on "why" he had created this document. Thanks to this, it was easy for my client not to second-guess himself when a couple of employees challenged the document, and to, instead, stick to the policy.

How much training do your employees receive on hiring? Who trains them?

What's your follow-up system to be sure they've absorbed and implemented everything they learned and are doing everything the way you'd like it done?

What's your system for on-going training for your seasoned employees, to ensure that they're staying up-to-date with all of today's new technology?

How supportive are your employees? What would it take to turn them into a championship support team?

Case Study (continued)

In a communication workshop I led with the employees in the company I referred to above, I first heard from each of them how the business currently operates, and then how they would operate the business if it were theirs. We then compiled a list of recommendations that each and every one of these employees, in this small business, agreed they would like to pass along, through me, to their employer. The recommendations were:

1. for the employees to work more as a team
2. for the employees to be more supportive of their co-workers and
3. for the employees to be more supportive of their employer!

Employees never cease to surprise me with how supportive they truly want to be, yet they just can't bring themselves to be the leader of the group to create a system of support and implement it. In fact, the one other recommendation made by this group of employees, a request they had specifically for their employer, was to hear their employer show gratitude for the work they did for him. They wanted to hear the words "thank you" once in a while. The employees, in our workshop, however, explained that they understood why it would be so difficult for their employer to say "Thank you" to them because they felt like they were spending so much time complaining that it didn't leave a lot for their employer to be grateful for.

When I submitted my summary report of the Communication Workshop to their employer, he said "I can do this one," pointing to the request: Say "thank you". I questioned: "With sincerity?" After some reflection, he explained to me (and himself) how he *could* say it with sincerity because

a) this one employee had, by making a judgment call, saved the company several hundreds of dollars and saved the job time;
b) another employee had actually brought work into the business;

c)   another had trained a new hire without being asked, etc.

Yes, he certainly could, and then did, say "thank you" with sincerity—such that he told me, within the next 3 weeks that the guys were melodiously saying to their employer, on pay-day as they were receiving their wages, "Don't forget to say thank you!", causing my client to feel very thankful for the FUN having come back into the business from such a small investment. In fact, he told me that **the morale hadn't been this high** in so many years he couldn't remember when it last was!

Your employees don't want to work for overworked,
stressed and cranky people.

The Top 3 Problems in the Workplace Today

Hundreds of 1,000s of Canadian dollars were invested by Canada's Federal Government to have in-depth research conducted to determine what the Top 3 Problems were in today's workplace. The Top 3 Problems, as they were identified, are:

1.   Communication
2.   Respect
3.   Support

and in that order. Having also served businesses in other countries, I am in full agreement with this list, only I don't see these problems as being the Top 3 only in workplaces. I contend that Communication is the #1 problem period . . . in your family, with your service providers, people in your community, as well as your customers and your employees . . . simply with everyone, in every relationship.

On a scale of 1-10 how effective do you feel your communication is with your employees? And vice-versa? I contend that if we focus on improving our Communication that the issues of Respect and Support will simply dissipate; and over the last 8 years since having learned about these Top 3 Challenges, and making the recommendations to my clients to simply focus on improving Communication, I have ample proof that *it's as simple as that!*

One of the biggest challenges we do have in all businesses today is most definitely the Support Team. The young people of today simply are not the way the young people of our day were. They haven't been raised to show respect to their elders in the way that we were. Nor have they been raised to solve their own problems, to reason things out. Nor are you raising your children in that old-fashioned way. That doesn't make it wrong; it simply makes it different. It's almost like we're trying to play two different games at the same time, and who knows the rules of the game that you, the employer, are expecting your employees to play day-after-day?

This is where Communication comes in. Do you even know what the rules are of the game you're expecting everyone to play in your business? How frequently do you have meetings with your employees—in separate groups, depending on the departments, and with everyone together . . . in what I call a Town Hall Meeting, asking for their involvement, as well . . . in order to clearly communicate what the rules of the game are? I encourage you to have at least one meeting every month, and if you haven't had any in quite some time, start with having your 2nd meeting 1 week after the first meeting; and then another 2 or 3 (as deemed necessary) after 2 weeks each, followed by regular monthly meetings thereafter.

How, exactly, do I conduct these meetings? I'm always asked.

1. Start by creating what may be your first-ever written Staffing Policy. If you already have one, how up-to-date is it? This is your opportunity to not only ensure every employee has a copy of the most recent version of the Staffing Policy, but also to explain to them in very clear terms, ensuring everyone understands, both what the purpose of each policy is and the reason for implementing the policy.
2. What's in this Staffing Policy? The answer to every question an employee has ever asked, that's what. Furthermore, code of conduct goes in here. Acceptable behaviour descriptions go into this Staffing Policy. Just think of every issue you've ever had to bring up to an employee, since the start of being in business, and every issue you've wanted to bring up, yet haven't dared. These topics go into the Staffing Policy, and it's a living, breathing document that will be up-dated every single time an issue comes up.
3. Ask your employees for their opinions in these meetings, as well. After all, they're the ones doing what they do every day, you aren't. These are the people who deal with the issues you're tolerating, and no doubt some of your employees are frustrated about these issues as much as you are. How do they feel things would work better, go more smoothly?

These meetings truly are Communication Meetings, because they're not just for you to do all the talking, wondering if anyone is listening to you. They're also for them to participate. They may be reluctant in the beginning because, of course, they all have their preconceived notions of what "a meeting with the boss" is about. Do you remember being called in to the principal's office at school? So do they. And, of course, they've heard stories during their childhood of a parent, aunt or uncle, sibling, someone's company making changes to *the way things are done around here* and it resulting in people being fired or laid off. As I've mentioned earlier in this book, we all have an *operating system* and even though we're about to have an experience for the 1st time ever, we will paint it with the memory of a previous experience (even if it's an experience of someone else of which we've only heard the heated story—full of feelings/emotions); and so will you. Therefore, whenever you're starting a new system, new policy, it's essential to know that you will come up against this—from yourself and from the others involved, and therefore it's essential that you have the support to keep you going even when the going feels tough.

If you simply focus on improving the Communication in your business, your business will improve dramatically in very short order. You will feel you have more respect and support from your employees and your employees will become much more plugged-in than you ever imagined, because they now feel you respect them and that everyone on the team is supporting each other.

Feeling respected and supported goes a long way to improving the mental health in your business. Mental health in the workplace is quickly becoming the #1 workplace illness—soon to surpass heart problems. Sadly, however, mental health in the workplace has no age barriers. It affects everyone at every age and your company can start paying out, through your benefits, within weeks of an employee starting at your company. This is costly for you as the employer, of course, because not only are these people receiving costly benefits, but you also need to have the work completed for which you hired them in the first place, costing you yet another salary.

Let's focus on dramatically improving **COMMUNICATION** in your company, and that alone will see your business flourish through increased productivity, save you money which can go towards paying off your debts as discussed in the previous chapter and your increased profit easily goes towards creating the reserves I mentioned therein. **The bottom line really is dramatically improved simply through improving Communication.**

Ensuring your Instructions were Clearly Understood

One simple habit to develop when giving instructions to your employees is to ensure they fully and completely understand what they just heard you say. Instead of asking: *Do you understand?* to which there is only one correct answer, you ask them to *Kindly repeat back to me what it is you heard me say, so that I'm sure I was able to give you the instructions clearly (or explain the situation clearly*—if you're using this method to have a critical conversation with someone).

Now, when they tell you what it is they *"heard you say"* you may at first feel frustrated to hear that they *"weren't listening"*. In fact, they were listening—through their filters—to what *you* said through *your* filters. This is precisely how we normally speak. It's the *"he said/she said"* syndrome and it happens in nearly 100% of conversations. This is a way for you to break that cycle in your business.

When your employee hears something different than what you intended to convey—whether it's very different or only slightly different—it's imperative that you remain calm. Take this as a learning experience about the way you communicate. Is it only with your employees that you find you're not being understood? Or do you have the same situation in your family conversations, with your customers, on Committees?

When you've learned that your words were not understood in the way you desired, simply repeat your instructions, if they were clear in the first place, and again ask the listener to *Kindly repeat back to me what it is you heard me say, so that I'm sure I was able to give you the instructions clearly.* By using this choice of words your employees don't feel at fault and they then feel much safer to remove their filter and hear precisely what you're saying.

For any conversation to be effective, both parties must feel safe to speak and to be heard.

In an ideal business environment the following is the norm:

- ✓ The Principal appreciates the team and customers.
- ✓ The Team appreciates the principal, each other and the customers.
- ✓ Customers are selected for their ability to appreciate the team and principal.

How appreciated do the people on your team feel? Dare to ask them. You may wish to do this by way of secret ballot or otherwise, depending on the number of people on your team, but you do want to know, on a scale of 1-10, how appreciated the people on your team feel. That's a great place to start with your first Communication Team Meeting.

NOTE: Not everyone reading this book, nor all of my clients, have employees, but everyone does look to others for support, and the tips in this chapter work equally well with all of your support team—paid and unpaid.

In the book by James Parker, former CEO of Southwest Airlines, Do the Right Thing: How Dedicated Employees Create Loyal Customers and Large Profits, it is stated that employee engagement starts with senior management being willing to ask the following questions:

1. Do our employees feel valued and respected? _____
2. Do their opinions count? _____
3. Are they acknowledged for their contribution? _____
4. Do they know what is expected of them? _____
5. Do they understand the purpose of their work? _____
6. Do they know where the organization is going? _____
7. Do they feel cared for? _____
8. Are they told the truth—the good and the bad? _____
9. Is there a high level of trust within the organization? _____
10. Are they clear about the role they play in the company's success? _____

Your exercise: Score your company on each of these questions with a score between 0 and 10.

Then, DARE to give these questions to each and every one of your employees and ask them to score each question with a score between 0 and 10.

You don't want your employees to be overworked,
stressed and cranky people.

The Helium Game

Imagine that every human being is like a balloon. Inside the balloon is helium, which represents each person's self-confidence. When you add helium, the balloon expands and rises. Take helium out—it deflates and drops to the ground. ADOPT THE HABIT of only adding helium to other people's balloons. This is critical. Unless you have a 'Helium Culture' in place at your business, everything else will be irrelevant. It's the foundation upon which everything works.

Your Exercise: For the next week, play the Helium Game. Find a way to say or do something to another human being, which increases the amount of their helium or self-confidence. You could perform this experiment with your friends, employees, customers, family, bank manager, the person at the checkout in the grocery store—even the person who cuts in front of your car.

Why is this important?

- ✓ It makes you an extremely "attractive" person—and we attract to us who we are "being" on the inside.
- ✓ People will be drawn to you.
- ✓ Opportunity will be drawn towards you.
- ✓ Your own self-confidence will increase as a result.
- ✓ The atmosphere in your business will improve dramatically.
- ✓ Negative people will naturally move on and leave the business.

The Law of Attraction: We attract to us not "what we want" but WHO we are BEING at any given moment.

As the week progresses make a note, each day, of anyone to whom you consciously added helium:

Monday: _____

Tuesday: _____

Wednesday: _____

Thursday: _____

Friday: _____

Saturday: _____

Sunday: _____

> How did this exercise affect your perception? Document your findings:
>
> _____
> _____
> _____
> _____
> _____
> _____
> _____

Our Drivers—C.A.R.

On my website, www.mljcoaching.com, you will find a video training I've created, teaching on Our Drivers. It will require a lot more explanation and pages than we have here at this time. If you don't easily find it there, e-mail **info@mljcoaching.com** and it will be our pleasure to send you the link to the video.

The condensed version is that we all have different personalities, depending on our birth order, our upbringing, our past experiences, etc. There are many tools out there to identify the personalities of everyone in your company. This C.A.R. which I created a few years ago seems to be the most practical and easiest to understand. As with everything in my business, and in my life . . . *It's as simple as that!* If it isn't simple, it's too complicated to catch my interest and, in the last 20 years I've identified that "complicated" is what keeps most people from making changes to their habits, to *the way things are done around here.* So, let's **keep it simple**, shall we?

Our **DRIVERS** are our default system—they're what "drive us" to do what we do and to behave the way we do. We are all driven, to a certain extent, by all three of these simple drivers, but when under stress we automatically revert to our "default" driver. This is the Driver I will help you identify, in each and every one of the people around you—family, employees, customers—and eventually in yourself, too. It's easier for you to watch this video, to which I refer above, and to show it to one of your key employees and ask him/her to identify what drives you.

The purpose of learning about our Drivers is to ensure that you have the right person in the right job. Having the wrong person in a job means that day in and day out that person is working against their natural ability and strength. How frustrated would you feel at the end of every day if every single day you felt like you were pushing boulders uphill—not having a lot of fun nor accomplishing very much? Maybe you do feel this way. It's relatively easy for you, then, as the business owner, to simply hire people to do all of those tasks you don't enjoy doing—those tasks that require the most effort—allowing you to work in your brilliance, doing those tasks that come so easily to you—where you shine, where you're having fun, feel accomplished and where you see so many beneficial results.

On the other hand, if your employees feel frustrated and unsuccessful at the end of the day, is there any wonder they're not very pleasant people to be around? Is there any wonder, if they're constantly pushing a huge boulder uphill, why even though they seemed to be the ideal candidate when you hired them, they're now leaving for another job?

Do be sure to check out that video which you'll either find at **www.mljcoaching.com** or by sending us an e-mail at **info@mljcoaching.com** and we'll be delighted to send you a link to it.

How *do* you Lead a Championship Support Team?
By becoming a *Championship Leader.*

For many people it feels very uncomfortable to apply some of these exercises with their employees. I encourage you, as I do my clients, to start practicing the new systems on

*your children. You, too, will see immediate benefits in your family time, and you will feel
much more confident when using these exercises with your employees, of course, resulting
in wonderful benefits in your business, too.*

Empower your Support

I've explained how you can become a Championship Leader, through improved Communication,
show of Respect and being truly Supportive.

"How do I Empower my Support?" you may be asking.

One of the biggest challenges for employees today is that they are not being developed in the
way that is essential for their own personal growth. *Everything* is subject to the Law of Expansion.
Your employees, therefore, must also expand in their personal and professional development.

It's not easy, however, for a small business owner, who likely started your business as a self-
employed person, to hand the reins over to these people who you find so challenging to
understand. Nonetheless, it's imperative that you do so.

Do you remember when your children were growing up? It wasn't easy to hand them new
responsibilities, either, especially if those responsibilities had crucial outcomes for the family
or for your child. Your alternative is to keep your employees from growing, keep them at the
level they're currently at . . . and you will find yourself like a person who was sitting in the
front row of one of the workshops I conducted a few years ago.

> *"I have no challenges hiring people. I've hired 20 people for the same position in the last 4 years.
> My challenge is finding "good" people."*

As we looked at the type of people he was hiring and how they developed in the short time
they were with him, it was clear to see that he wanted "gofers"—not employees. He hired
people for their skill and then he only gave them errand jobs: *"Go for this"; "Go for that".* Is
there any wonder these people gave less and less to their positions in a short period? They had
expectations, as well, of what this position was going to provide to them (far more than just the
wages) and within a few months of doing nothing but running errands and cleaning up after
their superiors they saw they were wasting their time.

A guide I have found helpful over the years in up-levelling the responsibility being given to an employee, to ensure that I am "empowering" my support, which comes from Stephen Covey's book, *First Things First,* follows:

New-Hire's AUTHORITY TO ACT (Level of Competency / Initiative):

1. Wait until told.
2. Ask.
3. Recommend.
4. Act and report immediately.
5. Act and report periodically.
6. Act on own.

NOTE: I recommend you hand this sheet to each New Hire with a specific date at each level, above, indicating the date of the new hire's first (and next) performance review, in order to assess whether it's time to up-level the new hire to the next level. Again, this is Communication. The new hire sees immediately where (s)he can go to in this position, and by when (s)he's expected to get to the next level. It gives your new hires something tangible to work towards and look forward to.

Hiring Criteria

To date, I find that the most common factors looked for in new hires are their experience in performing the tasks you have for them. Did you know that that's the easiest part of your job—to teach them how to do the tasks you want to hand off to them . . . or the tasks of the person they're replacing? If the candidate has the ability to learn—aptitude—then (s)he will quickly learn how to do these tasks . . .

*IF . . . they have the right **ATTITUDE**.*

Therefore, I recommend you hire people for ***ATTITUDE*** and, of course, a certain amount of aptitude. The experience will come quickly, ***with the right attitude***. Even large-sized "small" businesses, with 8-10 different departments and 50-100 employees, have been caught in hiring *the perfect person for the job*, because the person told them how good (s)he was at the job. Within weeks they were dealing with good, solid longer-term employees quitting because of the "holier than Thou" attitude of this new hire, who seemed to management to be perfect for the job.

There is NO replacement for training. Even if you do hire someone who seems to have a fabulous attitude, and years' experience in your type of work, this person has never before worked in your business. Regardless of how good you feel they are and how good they feel they are, there is no excuse for not Training them on *the way things are done around here!*

Probation Period

As I write this book, I'm touring Australia where they, too, have a probationary period for new hires. In most, if not all, provinces in Canada our common period of probation is 90 days, unless negotiated with the employee. You may be surprised to learn that of the several hundred small business owners with whom I've been in partnership over the last 10 years, more than 90%, before our working together, never marked the 90-day deadline of the probationary period in their agendas. Why would they? So that they would *know* if this was an employee to whom they wanted to offer permanent employment. Also, so they could celebrate their permanent employment status at or near the 90-day mark.

Since helping many small business owners use this employment law to their benefit, there have been many new employees who were offered an extended 90-day probation period. Sadly, most of them were then replaced before the end of that 2nd 90-day probation period, but it made my clients feel "nicer" as people to give them a 2nd chance. This exercise also helped each one of the employers to be diligent during the 1st 90-day period, and to release new hires that just aren't interested in following the systems at your place.

*Statistics show that it takes **9 months** for small business owners to release an employee!*

Sadly, on hearing that statistic, above, I looked back over my years of being in business and found that the statistic was spot on for MLJ Coaching International, as well. Therefore, suffice to say, that the moment you question the employee's loyalty, honesty, ability, attitude, whatever . . . release them then and there, or at least take *immediate* steps to replace that person then and there. I can assure you: 9 months later you will, finally, be letting that employee go after having spent and lost a lot of unnecessary money, time and emotion. Therefore, *j.f.d.i* . . . . *now!* (www.jfdi.ca)

*Empowering your support is **KEY** to **getting the FUN back into your business**.*

CHAPTER SEVEN

Your Customers Pay for Everything, right?

Strategy # 6
GET REFERRALS from **IMPRESSED CLIENTELE:** Help your Customers market your business for you

Again, it's very simple. We start by impressing our clientele. Most of the people with whom I enter into partnerships to grow their businesses already have a solid database of customers. Therefore, we simply start by analyzing that list—grading the customers. There are 2 ways in which to grade the customers. The first is to look at your customers from your point-of-view, identifying whether or not to continue to work with these customers. Secondly, we look at your performance from your customer's point-of-view and identify your vulnerable points. By daring to eliminate tolerations, you'll find that your business will attract the type of clients you want to work with. (Remember the Law of Attraction: We attract to us who we are BEING at any given moment.)

If you happen to be in need of an influx of cash to your business right now, you'll want to open your agenda and dedicate 2 hours to completing the following exercise. It's very simple to get cash flowing *into* your business and you'll see results almost immediately. I swear: You'll see results of *cash flowing into* your business *immediately* if you follow these instructions to the letter.

Immediate Cash-Flow Case Study

I'd been giving these instructions to clients for a few years already when the best example of how effective they are came along, shocking many other small business owners who were participating that day in the tele-seminar program, *7 Simple Strategies 4 Success,* in which they all heard one gentleman's dilemma. We were currently focusing on **Strategy #3: Follow Through** when a participant spoke up and said:

> *"Lynne, it's pretty hard to follow through on my plans towards my 3-year vision these days. Down here in Southern California our economic winter (as I refer to it) has gone into a deep-freeze! I have absolutely **no work** and it looks like I'm going to have to let go of all the rest of my employees. I've already pared them down to only having the best still working with me, and once I lose them I know they'll find work elsewhere and that doesn't look very promising for the future of my business."*

Wow! What a dilemma! This gentleman had been in a full-day workshop with me that took place just a few months earlier where we covered every single one of my **7 Simple Strategies 4 Success** so I excused myself to everyone else in the program, saying *One day this could be you, and it doesn't have to be, so listen closely.*

I encouraged this gentleman to pull out his workbook from that day-long workshop he'd attended and review his ideas that he'd written down when he was listening to me training on the strategies. In particular, I encouraged him to review his own ideas on how to GET REFERRALS, or whichever actions he made notes on regarding this Strategy that spoke to him. Then I reminded him to grade his database of customers; call up 10 people on the "A" list before the end of that day and make luncheon appointments with them over the next 10 business days. Then, going through the "B" list put names into his agenda to stop in and see a "B" customer on his way to meet an "A" for lunch, and to stop in and see another "B" customer on his way back to the office, after having dined with his "A" customer.

Two weeks later, when I heard this gentleman join the tele-seminar I immediately asked him how things were today with the grave situation he'd shared with us 2 weeks earlier.

> **"Well, Lynne, I had two lunches, received 4 jobs and now my biggest problem is that I don't have enough manpower to get all 4 jobs done!!!"**

We could all hear it in his voice. He was beaming from ear-to-ear! So, should you ever require a cash injection into your business,

It's as simple as that!

Cash-Flow Case Study

Another gentleman was telling me that, hearing this story, above, he decided he'd apply it with stopping in to reconnect with customers he hadn't seen in some years. He used another suggestion, which was to give them a gift card for a very popular coffee shop. In one week he distributed four gift cards each worth $20 and from one person, on the spot, he received one job worth $4,000 profit. Because of the situation this gentleman was in he was able to complete that job that week. Talk about a cash injection! He invested $80 to receive $4,000—profit, not the value of the job, but $4,000 in profit. That's an ROI of some 5,000%—neither 5%, nor 50%, nor even 500%. That's one serious ROI. Was it luck? In my world there's no such thing as luck. What we focus on we create. *It's as simple as that!*

Did he feel comfortable doing this? He told me that he struggled with himself *for a few months*, even, before he finally did it, so he most certainly did not feel comfortable doing it. It took him, as we say, *"out of his comfort zone"* but the $3,920 profit was not *inside* his comfort zone, was it? By daring to do something his subconscious mind had been successful in talking him out of doing until that week, he cleared $3,920. How much discomfort are you willing to feel for that kind of money, knowing that it's growing your business and helping you and your family?

Grading your Customers

Using the A, B, C and D method, which I find simple, I encourage you to grade your existing customers as follows:

"A" Customers are **GOOD** to work with and have lots of money. (Because I'm Canadian I use a "dollar" symbol to show this. It could be that your currency is Euros, Pounds Sterling, Won, Yen, or whatever else, so feel free to change the symbol to work for you.)

A　　　　GOOD　　　　 **$**

"B" Customers are equally **GOOD** to work with. It's just that they do not have lots of money. They are still **GOOD** to work with, remember, meaning they work *with you* on your customer delivery systems, not challenging every item in your agreement.

B   **GOOD**   **$**

"C" Customers, on the other hand, are not so good to work with for whichever reasons. Maybe you have to chase them for money; they expect to get more work done than the contract states; they don't want to sign contracts; they want things done *their* way with little or no regard for you and *the way things are done around here*, in your business.

If you refer back to the previous chapter, covering your Championship Support Team, you'll remember something I said there that equally applies in this chapter:

In an ideal business environment the following is the norm:

- ✓ The Principal appreciates the team and customers.
- ✓ The Team appreciates the principal, each other and the customers.
- ✓ Customers are selected for their ability to appreciate the team and principal.

"C" quality Customers oftentimes do not seem to appreciate your team or you. "C", in this case, stands for "**Change**". These customers belong in one of the other 2 categories—A or B—by default. They should only continue to be your customers because they are **GOOD** to work with and, by natural default, they either have a lot of money or they don't have a lot of money but they are still **GOOD** to work with, because they appreciate both your team and you.

C   **CHANGE**   (to **A** or **B**, where they rightly belong)

For the purposes of creating an influx of cash we don't concern ourselves with the "C" customers, except to be sure not to bother to have lunch with them, nor to stop in and visit them on your way to and back from lunch. For the purposes of growing your business, however, you may decide that one or a few of these "C" customers are worth the investment of your time, energy and emotion to give them the opportunity to become an "A" or "B" customer again, as I'm sure they were when they first became one of your customers. In this instance, it's up to you to decide right now, how far gone these "C" customers are. It's also important for you to recognize that you are the one who turned them into a "C" customer if, in fact, they were an "A" or "B" when you first invited them into your business, because they were good to work with.

There are cases where they were "C" customers—ie. disrespectful of you, your team or your systems—right from the get-go, but for one reason or another you chose to tolerate their behaviour. You taught them, therefore, that the way they wanted you to do things was acceptable, rather than you insisting on this customer following *the way things are done around here*, in your business. This often happens if these were customers we partnered with before we had our systems in place. We may have accepted them as customers because we needed the money. We know better now, and we have more confidence in the quality of work we do or products we sell. We no longer "need" to tolerate that type of behaviour. Sylvio of LeBlanc Custom Homes gives us an example of this at **http://mljcoaching.com/case-studies/ trade-contractors-business-success**. Again, as I said earlier, it's up to you to decide the value of having a critical conversation with this customer to let them know that they must adhere to *the way things are done around here* for their benefit in getting their job done properly. If they choose not to change or if you choose not to bother to help them become an "A" or "B" customer, then they simply become a "D" customer and you Dump them . . . immediately. I don't mean you should do this with any rancour. After all, you're the one who taught them to behave this way with you and your company, your team, yourself. Remember Sylvio's story, above? Therefore, I recommend you have a list of 3 businesses that provide services or products similar to what your business provides and the next time this "C" customer contacts you to become your customer again you simply remind them of your critical conversation if you had one. If you didn't have that critical conversation you simply explain that you don't feel your business would be the best solution for their need and refer them to the 3 businesses you have on the list. In fact, your receptionist can just as easily do this on your behalf.

"But can't we just hang onto 1 of these "C" customers? Yes, they're a pain, but we do make a good chunk of money off of them . . . eventually."

Of course you can! I don't tell anybody what they may and may not do. After all, it's your business. I'm simply making recommendations; simple recommendations based on results— desired results. Let me explain why I recommend you rid your company of "C"-quality customers.

C   **CHANGE** to become **A** or **B** (above)   . . . or . . .

D   **DUMP**

First of all, "C" customers demand a lot more of your attention and most of that is negative attention. This exhausts you and leaves you frustrated. On whom do we take out our frustrations? Our customers? That wouldn't be a prudent thing to do, now, would it? No, we take our frustrations out on those who are nearest and dearest to us—if not our family members then our employees. Why should they get the brunt of your continuing to tolerate a customer who you know you should be "D"-ing right now without even asking yourself the question about keeping them on?

Secondly, the purpose of this Strategy is to GET REFERRALS, right? Have you ever heard the expression:

Birds of a feather flock together?

All of these expressions of wisdom come from experience. So your business continues to have "C" Customers—if only just 1—as pillars of your business. You want referrals from all of your customers. When you ask your customers for referrals they will refer you to people *just like them*. Get the picture? Asking a "C" Customer for a referral means that you're now bringing more "C" customers into your business. And knowing that they're *not* **GOOD** to work with, why would you want to? Furthermore, keeping "C" customers in your business runs the risk of these c-omplainers rubbing shoulders at a dinner party with one of your "A" or "B" customers and if you've ever heard anyone complaining then you know that it's easy for the non-complainer to get caught up in the negativity and now you'll have a **good** customer turning into a "C". Furthermore, I've found that the most unsolicited referrals come from "C" customers, and why wouldn't they? When their friends learn what all you'll tolerate they want some of that "bending over backwards," too.

Customer–Dumping Case Study

Over the years, I have worked with many a good person who just felt they couldn't *let go* of a couple or even one "C" customer . . . until they finally did. One such story comes from a business in the construction industry. There had been an accident on a jobsite with absolutely no fault whatsoever on the part of my client's company, but performing his due diligence he visited his lawyer, nonetheless. Even the lawyer felt that there was no wrong–doing or negligence on the part of my client's company, yet several weeks later my client received a letter from the lawyer for the General Contractor. It took some costly doing and time to get there, but it was eventually seen by the General Contractor, as well, that my client's employee was not at all at fault.

Less than 2 years later another incident occurred with this same client of mine. This time, again with no fault on the part of my client's company, the situation involved many experts and took up a good lot of time and anxiety of my client. In one of our coaching sessions I asked something to the effect of what the common denominator was between these two incidents. The reason for my asking this is because I know that absolutely everything in our lives is created and attracted to us by *ourselves*. So, what was the cause of my client again attracting this situation to him and his business . . . and to his valuable employees?

"Common denominator?" he asked. "Well, it's the same General Contractor! Do you think this has something to do with him? Now that you mention it, I've been asking myself why any time I've ever had a serious situation it's always from a job with this general. Why do you think that is?" We very quickly identified that this general was a "C" Customer and had been identified by my client as such as soon as he heard me talking about "A", "B" and "C" customers more than a year earlier. Yet, he never once mentioned this one to me as one he "should" fire because he could always count on getting work from him. Sure he could. And this is what most of those jobs turned out to be like. Add to that frustration, fear, anxiety, stress, the fact that my client would wait 9 months to 2 years to get paid by this General, too, because he had the habit of dragging the end of the job out for so long that it would take forever to have the job finalized allowing the General to delay the need to make the final payment. My client got through that mess, was on Cloud 9 when telling me that all of the experts dragged in by both parties' insurance companies reported in my client's favour, and my client also exclaimed that he would never again take on a job for this General again. He said he even had the courage to tell him so at the end of the investigation. Again, as I recommend, with no rancour or hard feelings he simply stated something to the effect that there'd been enough strife between them that it would be best if the General never look to my client again to join him on a project. The General agreed as they parted ways that day.

As with every other *idea* that comes your way, I recommend that you act on it *now*, as the idea comes to you. If you have had an idea of hanging onto just one or a few "C" customers, as explained in the earlier chapter wherein I was training on Strategy #3: Follow through, hang onto these "C" customers at the expense of some "A"s and "B"s. If you choose *not* to step into what your intuition is telling you about the *idea* that just came to you, you will wish, within just a few months to a year, that you had. You can mark my words on it. Go ahead. Mark it in your calendar now. Hence, again, I recommend: www.jfdi.ca—*Just friggin' do it . . . now!*

Do you have IMPRESSED CLIENTELE?

Above, we're dealing with creating an influx of cash into your business through existing customers who, no doubt, you contacted first because you *know* they are impressed clientele. How about those about whose opinion you're uncertain? We both know you won't be contacting them right away for lunch, or to stop in and say "hi" on your way to and back from lunch with your impressed "A" customers. Everyone has customers in their database who they can say for sure were either not impressed or unimpressed. Is this due to lack of service or care on your part, or the part of your business? Or is it because they're "C" customers and they are unlikely to be happy with any service provided to them?

Have you ever asked your customers for their feedback? If not, this is a great time to start doing so. There are a variety of questions you'll want to ask your customers—your solid "A"s, "B"s and "C"s as well as your questionable ones. These questions come from you, your business, asking what you want to know about where your services could be improved, etc. I'm sure a quick Google of "customer feedback form" will give you ample ideas, and I also recommend you keep your eyes peeled for small businesses that serve you and some of the frustrations you, as a customer, have with them. I will, however, leave you with two essential questions that are very often missing in feedback requests from small businesses, recommending that you add these 2 questions to every feedback form you ever send out:

1. Thinking about all of your experiences with <name of your company>, thank you for grading your overall satisfaction in being served by us, where 10 is very satisfied and 1 is very dissatisfied.

   1   2   3   4   5   6   7   8   9   10

2. How likely are you to recommend <name of your company> to a family member, friend or colleague, where 10 is very likely and 1 is very unlikely?

   1   2   3   4   5   6   7   8   9   10

In response to Question 1, above, should you score less than 7, you'll want to have a system in place for these past customers to be contacted almost immediately so that you or someone fairly high-ranking in your business can get to the bottom of *What would have had to have happened in order for you to grade our services (or products) as 9 or 10?*

In response to Question 2, whenever you're in need of an influx of cash flowing into your business, the customers who scored higher than a 7 on their likelihood of recommending your business to a family member, friend or colleague will be contacted by you or the sales person who served them. If their score was 6 or lower, you will want to ask *What would have to happen for you to recommend us to a family member, friend or colleague?*

My main point here is that this feedback is gathered for the purposes of strengthening, improving and growing your business. Ensure that you make good use of it.

> ### *Did you know . . . that a disgruntled customer made happy is 20x more likely to recommend your services to others?*

That statistic almost makes you want to tick off some customers, eh, so they'll be 20 times more likely to sing your praises? Seriously, though: Ideally, you have a system, right from the prospective customer's 1st contact with your company, straight through to the end when they're feeling really good about the quality of work done for them, such that they're singing your praises to everyone who'll listen. When it comes to asking for referrals, yes, we ask because this is the only way we'll know to whom they're singing our praises. By daring to operate your business differently than the "norm" out there, you will dare to receive results through your business that far exceed the "norm".

It is not true that every client/project is won only on price!

Case Study

Your exercise, therefore, is to analyze your **Customer Flow System** and identify where improvements need to be made. One high-end service provider found that he was so excited about the work he did, the way in which he served his customers, that he would drive 2-3 hours to meet prospective customers at their place so that he could get a good scope of the work they wanted done. He'd excitedly talk with them for a couple of hours and even, at times, he realized in looking back that he'd been drawing sketches for the services he saw that they required. Then, another 2-3 hours back home . . . only some months later to learn that they decided to do it themselves or to hire someone whose rates were cheaper. What this gentleman realized, as we worked together, was that he was giving them a very clear picture of his vision for solving their problem, yet because his company wasn't the one carrying out the service these people in all likelihood ran into numerous problems in executing what they thought he was giving them as they saw him making the sketches. Furthermore, because of his "high-end" service, most of these people hadn't been qualified, to know if it was even something they were likely to pay for before this gentleman went off, in his excitement, for that full day to meet with them.

One of the first exercises this small business owner did as we worked together towards growing his business was to create a whole new *Customer Flow System*, right from the prospective customer's 1st phone call to his receptionist. He created questions for her to ask in that very first phone call and depending on their answers a telephone appointment may have been arranged for my client to speak with them . . . *by telephone*. If a prospective customer had shown interest at a trade show, a series of questions were asked of them *by telephone* following the trade show. This saved several hours that had been spent driving to and fro, and giving the farm away, allowing this entrepreneur much more time for *business development planning* (as in Strategy #2), which then caused his business to more than double inside of just 5 months.

Marketing 101

When I first started into business for myself, studying everything I could get my hands on, I consistently & persistently heard about *Sales & Marketing*. In fact, just within the last few months I was reading a book given to me by a client and I was surprised to still read that phrase: *Sales & Marketing*. Obviously that author had never heard my spiel on *Marketing & Sales*.

What is Marketing? Marketing is creating awareness *out there* of the way in which you, through your business, serve your community.

What is Sales? Sales is reaching an Agreement between a person or company that has a problem and you or your company, because you can solve this problem through your or your company's expertise, in exchange for an agreed upon sum of money.

Do you see, therefore, that we cannot have *Sales* without first *Marketing* your business, your service, your products? The *Marketing* can be as simple as filling your coffee cup at a networking event and exchanging pleasantries with a person who's also filling his or her coffee cup, explaining to each other what both of you do. The other person could say: *I've been looking for you! You see, I have this problem.* Therein you could make a sale, but you couldn't make that sale until this person knew the way in which you serve your community . . . by solving problems such as (s)he currently has.

There are various simple ways to market your business, but it's essential that you understand that marketing is all about relationships. Marketing is not necessarily advertising. Advertising is a marketing tactic, as is joining a networking group, as is writing a book, weekly newsletters, doing presentations to your niche market, making "friends" through social media, etc. Even if I were selling refrigerators, even though everyone in my community knows the benefits of them and requires at least one refrigerator in their home, if they know nothing about me they're more apt to purchase their refrigerator from a business owner they do know, or at least a well-known and reputable franchise. Marketing is all about relationships—including the sale you just made while pouring your coffee at a networking event, as I mentioned above. In your presence, that person you just met felt good vibes from you and, most likely, the problem isn't so large that your new customer feels he needs 3 or 4 testimonials and 3 or 4 other service providers for comparison and testimonials for them. At the end of the day it always comes down to ***relationships***. This is why creating and, most importantly strengthening, relationships with your customers and their referred friends, family members and colleagues is so vital for the growth of your business.

Just a few of the ways in building relationships, even when you're unaware you're doing it, is through **First Impressions**. You can only ever make but one *First Impression*. Be very mindful of your corporate image: How do you and your employees present yourselves, your tidiness, clothing, punctuality, cleanliness, likewise for your vehicle, your perceived organization if you're handing over written material to a prospective customer; your business facility if people's first contact with you is in an office; the tone of the voice answering their calls; right down to the condition of your business card which you fish out of the bottom of your purse or pocket in your vehicle.

NOTE: While I'm no expert in the **social media** world, I have been experimenting with various platforms and I've also done some research. I have a presence out there and I invest time into connecting with people through social media, however my research has disclosed my assumptions to be true: Some small business owners invest upwards of 20 hours/week and are still "hoping" they will one day make a sale they can attribute directly to social media "relationships". I contend that while you can meet many people easily through social media platforms, until you have voice-to-voice or person-to-person contact/conversations with them, there is no relationship and you're nothing more than a "bing" on their computer screen.

Sales 101

The most challenging issue for small business owners is becoming good sales people. For myself, in the early days, this was the position I was most wanting to hand off to someone much more capable than myself. I was willing to pay a much more handsome commission than most businesses offer—because I was so desperate to off-load SELLING. And then something magical happened. I learned that

> **SELLING ISN'T** *something we do* **TO** *people.* **SELLING IS** *something we do* **FOR** *people.*

Selling is not brow-beating, nor a gladiator contest. We help people make informed decisions to purchase what we offer . . . *because they have a need for or services/products.* Therefore, the first thing in a sales conversation is for us, the sales people, to determine whether or not they have a need or burning desire (strong want) for what we offer. If they don't, the conversation ends there. If they do, it is our duty to help them see that we have precisely what it is they want. This is not the place for me to delve deeply into the subconscious mind's workings on holding your customers back from easily making the purchasing decision, but I do want you to understand that scientific research has shown that *physical pain* is felt whenever people make a decision to spend money. In fact, it's the same amount of pain to spend $0.99 as it is to spend

$9,999. *Physical pain!* Yet, by their not moving forward into purchasing the solution you have for their problem, they will continue to feel a lot of stress, frustration, unhappiness, anger possibly to continue tolerating their problem; whereas by moving forward into purchasing the solution you provide they will only feel the same amount of pain as they will when they are making a purchasing decision for a chocolate bar. How much long-term stress, frustration, unhappiness, etc. will the purchase of the chocolate bar remove? How much stress, frustration, lack of happiness will your service or product remove? Come to know this, and to **understand** it, and you will then be able to easily help many more people see that your solution is what they want . . . and your business will SOAR in ways you never thought possible . . . simply because you came to understand that . . .

*SELLING is something we do **FOR** people.*

Some internal and external marketing tactics that I've been recommending for several years now are every bit as effective today as they have been since the beginning of businesses. On reviewing the lists, below, simply decide which ones you have and want to up-date or revise and which wants you don't have and want to create. These are all very *simple* marketing tactics, helping you *create awareness* or *heighten* awareness of your business and while, yes, there are more tactics than this, such as internet marketing, social media marketing, etc., it may be that just by improving what you're already using will have your business **SOAR** to the next level.

INTERNAL MARKETING TACTICS

1. Grade Existing Customers — Categories A, B, C and D
2. Create a Menu — of what your business offers (on your business card, in your portfolio, on your website)
3. Produce a Portfolio — showing your work to Prospects
4. Develop a Referral System — to have a constant flow of Prospects
5. Distribute Referral (Business) Cards — to facilitate the sending of Prospects to you

EXTERNAL MARKETING TACTICS

1. Fill your Reservoir of Prospects — with nearly everyone you meet, at networking events, your sports club, trade shows, Industry Association events, etc.

2. Networking	– Join your local Chamber of Commerce or Associations serving your niche market—and attend their events!
3. Public Speaking	– to your niche market at their Association's dinner meetings, golf tournaments, trade shows
4. Develop Strategic Alliances	– with someone who has the same customers in the same market as yours.
5. Create a Website	– It's far better to have a 1- or 2-page *classy-looking* site than a multi-page amateur-looking site. We all have a youngster in our entourage who knows how to create websites. Refrain from the temptation to do this on the cheap. Hire a professional whose work is very appealing to the eye.

This can't be stressed enough: **SELLING** *is something we do* **FOR** *people.*

CHAPTER EIGHT

Enjoy the Journey . . . Rest, Relax & have TONS of FUN

Article published in a trade magazine in January 2010:

★ ★

On the 14th day of being in Las Vegas, for one event after another, while in the airport on my way back home, I started writing the following article . . . focusing on

Strategy # 7
GET A LIFE (outside of the business). **Love what you do. Do what you love.**

The article almost completed, I check my luggage, get my boarding pass and start heading towards my gate. Along the way I see a couple I had just been chatting with in the check-in line-up and we continue our conversation.

Ditch the earlier article I was going to submit for publishing in this issue!

Instead, let me tell you Connie's and Brian's story. Sadly enough it's not so different from many others' stories.

Case Study of 3 Wake-Up Calls

Connie tells me she's pretty much fully recovered from a stroke that happened just 7 months earlier and this is the reason they're in Las Vegas. It was a long-time dream of hers and she nearly lost the opportunity to realize it. Connie's all of 42 years old and the mother of a 9-year-old boy*!*

As Connie told me about how suddenly her stroke happened, while out shopping with a girlfriend (whose recent experience of a stroke by an older family member actually saved Connie's life), I thought of a video I had just seen that morning in the conference.

There is no such thing as co-incidence.
Every "chance" event/meeting happens in perfect divine order.

While watching that video just that morning, about a young scientist, specializing in brain functionality, who had suffered a stroke around the age of 37, I was taken back to a very memorable time in my own life. *I was 28.*

I was cycling with my older daughter, then 7. My 5-year-old daughter was at our neighbour's house. As I was coasting down the hill my 7-year-old called "Mommy! Wait up." I looked back briefly and said "I'll wait for you at the bottom." *And did I!*

I turned my gaze back to the rural street ahead of me and only remember seeing our dog appearing from the woods, joining us in excitement. I remember calling out "Pajo! No!"

The next memory I have came 2½ days later. It was the feeling of excruciating pain as my then employer was (probably lightly, even) squeezing my hand. From there, as I was regaining consciousness, I remember even more excruciating pain in my head. Everyone was bothering me—loudly calling my name and asking me questions—dumb, insignificant questions, I remember, that they repeatedly asked. I was responding to them but it was as though they weren't listening to me. I then felt frustration, which mounted to anger as their incessant, loud demands continued whilst ignoring my responses. Little did I know that this was a tactic to keep my brain from shutting down completely, and little did I know that my speech was incomprehensible. I remember clearly telling myself "I'm tired anyway. I've been so tired lately and life hasn't been so pleasant, so I'm just going to take advantage of being in bed and go back to sleep."

In the days that followed, I experienced what Dr. Jill Bolte Taylor was describing (from the video in that day's conference in Las Vegas and which can be found on-line, as well) during the onset of her stroke, only in the reverse. The longer I was awake in those moments in the hospital, the more I saw that I was separate from my body. I and my body were 2 separate beings, it seemed. As the awakened moments lengthened we slowly became one again. By the end of one week I had sufficiently passed the barrage of tests to be allowed to go home to be with my babies again, but only because my doctors were assured I would have lots of support, with a sister-in-law staying with us. I still spent 23½ hours/day in bed for at least another week and, if I recall accurately, it was a good month before I was able to get out of bed in the mornings with my children and spend a couple of hours with them after school and in the evenings.

Why am I telling you these stories in relation to the **7 *Simple Strategies 4 Success*** on which I train and coach small business owners, to help you **EARN MORE PROFIT**, have **TONS MORE FUN**, and custom-build a **RETIREMENT** … on your terms, that's ready & waiting for the day you say *"Know what? I've had enough."*?

Let's go back to Connie & Brian in the Las Vegas airport, shall we?

Connie spoke repeatedly of how lucky she was.

There is no such thing as luck!

I explained to Connie that there was a reason why she had had that experience, including her survival and quick recovery. Her eyes nearly bugged out as they stared at me . . . almost in *disbelief!* Connie said "Actually, I think you're right, Lynne." In my confident, yet respectful way, I smiled and said "Connie, I know I'm right."

Connie told me something, in front of Brian, which left Brian speechless. Brian's shoulders weren't just slumped. He was bent forward; staring at his wife almost in disbelief . . . registering what he had just heard her tell a complete stranger in an airport.

Just days before Connie's stroke, Connie told me she had said "to the God" (her words) that she was fed up with the meanness and cruelty of so many people around them. If there were no more purpose to life than what she was feeling at that time she didn't want to continue living.

As Brian stood there in stunned silence, I assured Connie that she was right in her belief that she'd brought that stroke on to herself and that "the God" to which she'd pleaded clearly showed her that there is a purpose to her life—more than to just be the brunt of others' meanness.

And now it was Brian's turn to tap into the viewpoint of this stranger in the airport. Brian asked for my take on his work situation.

Classic example of being in a job where he'd given it his all, and proudly, for nearly ¼ of a century . . . and how he'd not only been passed over for a well-deserved and logical promotion, but how the new 28-year-old (son) boss wouldn't even speak to Brian anymore since informing Brian that he was no longer in the plans for the company's growth! What was my advice? Brian asked.

Not knowing that a good professional coach doesn't give advice, Brian wasn't ready to answer the question I posed:

"What would be the ideal situation for you, Brian?"

Brian responded with more explanations. I silenced him . . . and repeated the question.

Again, Brian tries to deflect the direct question, in his lack of confidence in having "the right answer."

"Brian! STOP!" I said, firmly, yet in a friendly manner, with my hand held up. "What would be the ideal situation **for you**?"

With a huge smile lighting up Brian's face, he says "I'd love to quit and start my own business. I've been doing this for years and I still love it. I just don't love the people I'm doing it for."

"And what's stopping you from quitting and starting your own business?"

The pay-cheque.

Connie interjects with "It's been such a stress on our life for all these 3 years and the doctors think it may be one of the things that contributed to my stroke. In fact, Brian feels guilty every day, thinking his negative attitude towards work has played a major role in causing my stroke."

"How much more of a wake-up call do you need, Brian? For these 3 years you've been waiting for this promotion and now for months you know you'll never get it. Your soul is dying every single day. The stress is literally killing your loved ones!"

What I recognized when I was again able to think and reason, after my head injury, was that there were so many things I hadn't yet done in my life. I, like Brian, had been settling for less . . . unhappily holding myself back, in accordance with someone else's fears.

Brian's settling, he knows, nearly cost him more than a marriage, but a loving wife . . . and the mother of his young son. Brian knows this, yet he still lacks the courage (which is simply faith in himself) to do what his soul is screaming at him to do: **Quit his job and start his own business.**

It's as simple as that!

I can't say that Brian made a decision right there and stepped into it, burning the ships to eliminate the possibility of retreat, but I know that as I ran to grab a sandwich before my flight home Brian had lots to think about on his flight back to British Columbia, Canada.

Can you now see how this story relates to **Strategy #7: GET A LIFE (outside of the business)**—Love what you do. Do what you love?

You are likely in business for yourself already. How satisfied are you . . . on a heart & soul level . . . with your business?

How many vacations do you take each year? And for how long are they (or is it)?

Do you know that it takes a minimum 2 weeks at least twice/year to recharge your batteries? Many of you tell me you'd get bored being on vacation for that long. Who said what your vacation has to be? In fact, I love adventures for my vacations. I have never before taken a 3-month vacation, such as the one I'm currently on living in a camping van touring Australia, but it's by no stretch of the imagination boring! As an entrepreneur I need vacations that totally sweep my mind away from the business . . . and so do you.

I don't expect you to start with a 3-week vacation right off the bat, but I do encourage you to set that as your goal. I highly recommend one 3- or 4-week vacation each year, as well as another 3 vacations for at least 5 days each. These can even be continuing education events, like trade-shows, annual association conferences, business workshops, product knowledge events. While those are not vacations, and should never be considered as such, you can always add a couple of fun days to both ends and you'll still come back refreshed from being in a different environment and stimulating your mind in different ways.

You also need to have customers who not only accept that you'll be away, but who feel confident that your powerful support team will serve them well . . . without being able to contact you while you're away. You will, of course, have set your business up with the types of customers who help you grow your business (Refer to Strategy #6).

"But we can't afford the expense of even one vacation every year, let alone more than one." This is a statement I hear all too frequently. Look at all of your other business expenses. You make them because they give you a good return on your investment, do you not? Vacations are the same. These are the times that you are fully recharging your batteries, reconnecting with your passion for the business . . . *getting back to why you ever got into business in the first place!*

Because you've focused on

- getting your prices right,
- budgeting for the family, as well as the business,
- being really clear on where you want your business and your lifestyle to be in 3 years' time,
- investing in **proper support** to make sure you follow through on your ideas while
  - planning business developments,
  - leading a championship support team,
  - hiring customers for their alignment with your business and lifestyle goals, etc.

then **GET A LIFE** (outside of the business) is actually a result of having focused on all of the other *7 Simple Strategies 4 Success* along the way.

I only mentioned 3 of us in this story with serious physical wake-up calls, but I know of so many more. One of them first became a client of mine after not only having had breast cancer, and a double mastectomy, at the age of 37, but after her 42-year-old husband had had a heart attack, following her last operation in that series. Lisa and Tim both recognize that their physical wake-up calls, while extremely unpleasant to experience, were the best things that ever happened to them, despite the fact that they had 2 young children who went through the experiences, as well.

PLEASE . . . BEFORE YOU GET A WAKE-UP CALL LIKE WE DID . . .

Start living your heart's desires today*!*

GET A LIFE *(outside of the business).*
LOVE WHAT YOU DO . . . *and* DO WHAT YOU LOVE!

I leave you with this exercise: When answering these questions, be honest with yourself . . . brutally honestly. Then make a decision on something you're going to do over the next 90 days . . . and break it down into tiny, manageable, bite-sized chunks, happily swallowing one of them every single day:

1. Sit quietly and reflect back to when you were making the decision to get into business for yourself. You may need to close your eyes to be able to go back that far. After all, a lot may have happened since then. In which year was it? In which season were you getting close to making the decision? What was happening at that time in your life? Where were you working? How old were you? Did you have children? How old were they? Where were you living? Which vehicle were you driving? The clearer you are of the scene, the more likely you are to really get in touch with your feelings at that moment. Can you remember?

2. What was the lifestyle you were dreaming of for yourself and your family at the time you were considering going out on your own? What, in particular, did you imagine the benefits of being self-employed would be? List them.

3. What was the type of
   - house you dreamed of owning?
   - vehicle you saw yourself driving?
   - adventures you'd be enjoying?
   - organization/association you imagined you'd be donating to, to give back some of your success?

4. At which age did you then imagine you would be retiring?

5. What was the income you dreamed you'd be taking home by now?

6. How many of these benchmarks have you reached already?

7. Accept that, while it goes against the culture of most of us, we have every right to earn whichever amount of money we desire . . . and with that money, we have every right to buy and enjoy whichever toys we desire. Believe it or not, this is one of the biggest components that holds us back from realizing most of the dreams we have.

Now, it's up to you. **Make a decision**:

1. What are you going to accomplish within the next 90 days to get you closer to where you want to be? Write it down.
2. Break it into tiny pieces and make a list of the pieces.
3. Keep this list in front of you every day for the next 90 days . . . and take at least one step every single day. No one's saying you're forbidden from lengthening the strides and increasing the pace!
4. If the "goal" is worth accomplishing, it's worth accomplishing within 90 days. **Get support! Proper support!**
5. Get back to the passion that you had for your business when you were just getting started. If you weren't passionate about it then, what would ever make you think you'd be passionate about it now? If this is the case, I encourage you to . . . like Brian . . . invest in yourself in order to light the fire in your belly.
6. Have **TONS** of **FUN** along the way!

★ ★

Above is an article that was published in a trade magazine in January 2010. As you've just read, included in that article are the "wake-up calls" for a few different people. Shortly after the issue of the magazine containing this article was published I received a message from a woman who had just read my article and wanted to talk to me to see if I could help them with their business results.

When Darlene and I talked a few days later she told me how serendipitous it was that she'd even read this article, because this particular article was the 1st one she'd seen of eight which were published in a series. It was the magazine that kept prompting her to pick it up, she said, instead of doing the usual and simply putting it into the pile of unread material in her husband's office.

After reading this article herself over lunch that day, Darlene insisted that Gene read it as well. She also took him onto my website. As Gene read a client's story on my website, **http://mljcoaching.com/case-studies/small-business-profits**, he wondered: *How can this man whose business I know of, but whom I don't know, possibly be telling my story?*

It still wasn't easy for Gene to do something he'd never heard of anyone he knows personally doing before, but he agreed to make what he felt was a sizeable investment and joined his wife in a VIP Intensive Coaching session, complemented with tele-seminar business strategies training and group coaching. Within a month, Gene saw from the value of the VIP Intensive Coaching session alone how the larger year-long program could be very valuable for them, especially given the four 2-day in-person training workshops. Left to himself, he knows he would *not* have joined this program, but he had the support of his wife to help him dare to go where few men have gone before—in admitting that

- they want more;
- that they're unable to do it alone; and
- that they're just not happy with their business anymore with *the way things are done around here today.*

Strategy #7—**GET A LIFE** (outside of the business). **Love what you Do. Do what you Love.**

This is the Strategy where we focus on you, the backbone of this creature to which you've given so much of your life. Have you ever had a sore back? How does the rest of your body feel when you're constantly feeling the ache of a bad back? This is the effect you, one person, has on the health of your business when you're not as strong as you need to be.

Strategy #7 is about prioritizing the key areas of your life such as

- Self
- Family
- Business
- Finance
- Physical and Emotional Health
- Social
- Intellectual
- Spiritual

And how do these get into your agenda? you may be wondering. By putting them in *!!! Simple as that.* As I mention above, you are the backbone of this creature to which you've given so much of your life and which has affected so much of your family's life. It's now time, past time, even, for you to **FOCUS** on the most important factor of a successful business: ***Its leader!***

We build on the reserves . . . of self, family, business, finance, health, social, intellectual and spiritual . . . and we eliminate the tolerations. After planning "free" days, we fit into them essential components such as

- ✓ nutrition
- ✓ sleep
- ✓ exercise
- ✓ reflective thinking
- ✓ and quality time   –   for the family, for the couple and for YOU!

And how do these activities get into your agenda? By putting them in. *It truly is as simple as that!*

CHAPTER NINE

FREEDOM: What's your Definition?

IT'S BEEN MY PLEASURE

One small business owner was explaining his generosity to me—of which I have no doubt. He doesn't hesitate to buy his wife a new vehicle if she asks for it, and his children have everything they've ever dreamt of. There was some irritation in his voice, however, as he was explaining this to me. So, why would he be so kind, generous, giving, even extravagant? Because he feels guilty, he says, for the time he doesn't spend with his family so he spends money instead. Sound familiar?

I know that many small business owners have an inner battle going on between the "old school" and today's families and workplaces. Our world has changed dramatically since many of us first started working and is in a state of constant, rapid change. It is my wish for you that this book be at least a great start in making things easier for you in dealing with those changes.

After Darlene and Gene had been working in a coaching partnership with me for fewer than 6 months I received this e-mail from Gene:

> "I was feeling anxious sitting on the fence on this decision (of stepping into the year-long coaching program). This session has given me a lot of clarity on moving forward with this big step that will definitely grow the business. I haven't had **FUN** in a long time and now with a taste of **4-day weeks** I didn't want to give them up. Right now I'm the **happiest** I have ever been running my own business. The Company has never run so **smoothly** and I don't want to lose that. I can see now that I don't have to, just to grow the business. (In our session I told him: "You won't give up your Fridays, **Gene**. We're going **forward** from here; not backwards.")

Lynne, your coaching has **enabled** us to make decisions more **quickly** and more **clearly** in the everyday operations of **PARALLEL ELECTRIC LTD.**, in order to focus on the bigger picture. The company's more rounded now that we're working with you, Lynne, than it ever has been before. I no longer feel guilty taking Fridays off and I might only get 1 call every other Friday from the guys. We're focusing on reducing those calls, even.

We're doing **so well** this year. We have been able to take **time off** to be a **family** more and **enjoy** more activities **together**. The Company has never run so **smoothly**. It was like it was running out of control before; like a vehicle going down the road with the **wheels falling off**.

I never wanted to do anything away from the business before; I'd gotten so **out-of-touch** with having **FUN**. This summer I've attended **more** classic car shows than ever before. And this winter I know I'm going to **finally** work on the classic I have in my garage."

Both Gene and Darlene continued to enjoy so many changes throughout that year, many up yet still some down, as they were working their way through their old programming. Then, nearly a year from this e-mail, above, I received another message from Darlene which they've also permitted me to share, in an effort to help everyone who, like themselves is stuck sitting on the fence in making the simple changes to get past their struggles, to simply *j.f.d.i.* and get off the fence:

Hi, Lynne

Gene has asked me to drop you a line to tell you how well this summer is going. Gene has said that his decisions are now quick, clear and precise thanks to your coaching. He has never felt more confident under so much pressure and we have TONS of work!! Our profits are very good and we are so grateful to you that all your wisdom is finally soaking in. Both Gene and I keep saying this month: "See! That is what Lynne was talking about!!" We see it now. It is much clearer. I guess we've just stopped resisting.

It is as if the veil has been lifted and the truth of your teachings are very clear now. It would be our pleasure to share this with others who are on the bridge towards understanding!

My point in sharing this recent message with you is to show you Gene's and Darlene's journey of working through the programming they grew up with, that for the most part they're still dealing with today. Our foundational "thinking" and "feeling"—our foundational operating system—isn't replaceable overnight. By sharing their journey with you, however, I'm hoping that you will see the benefit to you, your business and your family of working through each and every one of the exercises contained in this book.

Also, be sure to enter your contact information at **www.mljcoaching.com** and follow the exercises you'll find in my weekly newsletters, as well. On my website you'll find archived newsletters that I've been sending since 2004, most of which contain simple exercises to follow, of much the same simplicity as the exercises in this book.

The danger of the simplicity of my work is that people like you will "feel" it's so simple that it can't be very effective. We've been programmed to believe that the best things in life are the most expensive, the most difficult, the most complex. That's more of the programming of which I speak that keeps us playing small . . . much smaller than we were intended to play.

Dare to complete these simple exercises, in each and every one of these chapters, if you haven't already, and you will be amazed at the results you will receive. Gene and Darlene completed the Trade-Contractors' Business College program at the end of March and this message, above, was sent to me to in mid-July. They are still seeing the fruits of their labour . . . and so will you continue to long after you've completed the exercises in this book. And just like the workbooks each of my clients work through while in a coaching partnership with me, you have your very own workbook right here in your hands. Continue to work through the exercises year after year and there's absolutely no stopping you! You, too, will be turning your ship around within mere months and there's no reason why you would ever stop to SOAR with your business from there on in.

New Definitions of FREEDOM

As a result of coming to not only KNOW but UNDERSTAND my operating system, the foundation of which was created by me, in a flash, at the age of 5½, I now have a new definition of **FREEDOM**, which I've been enjoying since understanding and changing these limiting beliefs and feelings from my subconscious mind and this is precisely what the vast majority of my clients are focusing on creating for themselves. To me,

FREEDOM is NEVER looking at a PRICE-TAG again!

Consider that for a moment. How many times has the price tag made the purchasing decision for you? Taking you from about to purchase *what your heart desires* to **settling for less**.

One of my clients has a slightly different definition. In his words:

> *FREEDOM is being able to say, when the mood strikes me,*
> *"That's enough. I'm outa here!"*

We've only been focusing on that for 2½ years and he already has all of his ducks in-a-row and sooner than he could have ever imagined, he, too, will be living totally in **FREEDOM.** In the meantime, he's been on four 5-star vacations in less than a year for varying lengths—just for the couple, for the whole family and . . . just for him. So, until you fully reach *your* definition of freedom **HAVE FUN** practicing it*!*

As I've been travelling around Australia and conversing with people from other countries, as well, I continue to hear so much about the global economic crisis. I can assure you: Once you simply make a decision that there is no economic crisis in your business and in your family, then there won't be one . . . even if the media and those around you appear to have lots of evidence to the contrary. It's all an illusion.

> *What we FOCUS on . . . we CREATE.*

As my limo driver came to understand . . .

> *The BEST Investment you can make is in YOURSELF.*

It has been my pleasure to serve you throughout the writing of this book.

In signing off, I'll leave you with one more beneficial exercise:

When you've completed reading the remaining few pages of this book, invest 15 minutes to reflect on this question:

IF YOU WERE STARTING OVER right now with today's knowledge, what would you do differently?

Describe it—in detail. Do this in writing, remember. Writing it down dramatically increases the likelihood of your making these changes that you know will benefit you, your business and your family.

Then write down *one thing* that you *vow* to yourself to do—with a due date on it: either something you have only ever thought of doing before; or something you'll do differently from here on in . . . and then

Do whatever the heck it takes to j.f.d.i. !

Have FUN!

Lynne

P.S. Yet more wonderful news from Darlene (and I look forward to many more updates from them as both of their businesses and they continue to flourish):

> Lynne—Just leaving for vacation! Gene just shared this with me: "I have never felt so confident that I have left my business in very capable hands with a new dynamic team!" He has never felt so worry-free going on holidays!!
>
> We also have record profits this year :))))) Even better, he feels like he has gotten his power back!!!!!!
>
> He has really grown these past 6 months! So have I. I finally have my new business moving in the paying direction! Also, I am ready to get some video on my web and FB pages! My confidence is growing and my health is steadily improving.
>
> This really is a miracle. We have set our sails and marked our course. Thanks for getting us to make the map!
>
> Gene wants to thank you for your perseverance with him. He now sees he was being close-minded and stubborn. He is still working on this each day. He has broken through more things in 6 months than he has in his whole career!!!

We would not be on this holiday without you Lynne.

With great gratitude,
Darlene and Gene Paradis

And these words from the electrical contractor who you see in a video on my website on the testimonials page at **www.mljcoaching.com/testimonials**, who took his first 2-week vacation in 20 years . . . during the summer, the busiest season for an electrical contractor in his geographical area.

For me . . . **that's success!** Helping families such as Darlene's & Gene's in this way. What's *your* definition of success?

Just imagine: *If you were to* **MAKE A DECISION** *to take one small step in the direction of your 3-year vision **every single day**, where could you be 3 years from today?*

About the Author

The end of a phenomenal year in Lynne's small coaching business found her feeling tired. Wondering how to continue to grow her *fun* business without fatigue, Lynne stepped into further understanding small business growth through further developing herself. Lynne now helps her clients identify that "simple thing" that's missing and that "thing" that's stopping them . . . at an even deeper level than she had before. Quintupling her profits just a year-and-a-half from "feeling tired," Lynne helps her clients get the *fun* back into their businesses, and their lives outside of the business, while getting a start on their custom-built *retirement* . . . as double, triple, quadruple, even decuple the *profits* simply flow in the back door.